THE JOURNEY TO I DO

ELLANY T. KINCROSS

Photo credit: Ken Dapper Photography

Editing credit: Sue Ducharme, TextWorks

Copyright © 2013 Ellany T. Kincross

ISBN-10: 1481226894

EAN-13: 9781481226899

CONTENTS

INTRODUCTION

I am a third generation psychic, sensitive, and healer. My gift was passed along to me from my mother's side of the family. I have been doing readings and providing intuitive counseling sessions for more than fifteen years. I began receiving psychic impressions and premonitions at a young age. My most powerful and relevant premonition occurred when I foresaw the destruction of 9/11 the day before it happened.

For those of you who wonder, a reading is a meeting between a psychic and a client in which issues, challenges, and problems — physical, spiritual, emotional or a combination thereof — are discussed. During a reading, a psychic will explain the information she or he is receiving from Spirit, spirit guides, or angels. How do psychics receive this information? Psychics are very sensitive to energy. This sensitivity enables them to perceive energy in different ways. Psychics who are *clairaudient* can hear Spirit, spirit guides, and angels talking or whispering information to them. In this manner, psychics act as messengers who communicate what they hear. Psychics who are *clairvoyant* receive images or visions of events that have occurred in the past or that will happen in the future. Psychics who are *clairsentient* feel. Psychics who are

vi   THE JOURNEY TO I DO

claircognizant know, and psychics who are *clairgustient* taste or smell. Many psychics are a combination of the *clair-* types. I am mainly clairaudient, clairvoyant, and clairsentient; however, from time to time I have experienced clairgustient and claircognizant sensitivities during readings.

Similar to a psychic reading, an intuitive counseling session addresses a recurring issue, problem, or challenge that a client has faced over a period of time. For example, a client may be working through issues of grief over the loss of a parent. In such cases, the client will work with a psychic for a period of weeks or months until he or she attains healing with the issue.

A reading or an intuitive counseling session is a catalyst for changing an unsatisfying situation. Both a reading and an intuitive counseling session similarly provide a safe space for a client to express hopes, fears, dreams, regrets, joy, sadness, frustration, anger, and despair. In both types of sessions, the client can learn new tools and gather information about how to take the next step on her or his journey and begin to change the problem or situation. However, the willingness to take even the smallest baby steps is a prerequisite for both approaches. A client or a prospective client should meet with a psychic because he or she wants the current reality to change.

Psychic readings and intuitive counseling sessions occur in person or can be done over the phone. Due to the nature of their sensitivities, many psychics can connect with a client's energy over the phone. This is beneficial when clients live far away or in different parts of the US. I have conducted phone readings for clients as far away as South America and the East Coast. The energy is as strong over the phone as in person.

I have a unique approach to readings and intuitive counseling sessions. Most psychics give you the information they perceive. I give that information, but I also tie in the lessons you are here to learn, the way your soul needs to grow, and the importance of the evolution you need to attain in this lifetime. In other words, I focus on the journey you are here to take.

When you ask people about their hopes for their journey through life, they will often say that it is about finding the right career, the right partner, having children, and, hopefully, living happily ever after. Finding the right career is usually easy enough. However, when Mr. or Ms. Right is nowhere to be found, living happily every after can seem unattainable. For many people the journey to finding the right relationship and the right partner is often confusing, frustrating, and difficult. As a psychic, I can see the obstacles that are preventing clients from meeting the right person. What are those obstacles? Unfinished parental dynamics, unhealed emotions from previous relationships, a lack of understanding of what commitment entails, and the law of attraction at work in their dating choices.

The journey to the right relationship involves taking a series of steps that involve looking at who you are and what you desire in a relationship. Throughout the process of looking at yourself and everything that comprises who you are, a shift in your law of attraction occurs. Shifts in your law of attraction put you in alignment to meet the partner of your dreams.

As you embark on this journey, you'll become more connected with your true self. You will discover that emotions and feelings you have forgotten slowly bubble and rise to the surface as you work through the chapters in this book. These emotional expressions — tiny pieces of pain, sorrow, sadness, anger, and frustration —need to be healed. In healing these pieces of your inner puzzle, you'll find your way back to wholeness. The journey to wholeness can be beautiful, divine, and amazing. When you become more whole, you gain the ability to attract partners who radiate the same level of wholeness.

Somehow you were led to this book. Trust the guidance that brought you to this place.

I wish you a beautiful journey to the relationship of your dreams.

HOW TO READ THIS BOOK

I'd like to offer some guidance on the best way to read this book. The book is divided into three sections:

- The illusions of dating,
- Your inner work: Getting to the real you,
- Finding the right relationship.

Each section contains chapters that relate to the theme of the section. I recommend that the sections and the chapters within the sections be read in order. At the end of each chapter, the reader will find two exercises. They are:

- Key points for reflection and journaling
- A meditation to assist the journey

Upon finishing each chapter, the reader should take time to journal or reflect on the five *key points for reflection and journaling.*

The material in each chapter has been designed to stimulate the reader's thoughts. At the same time, the five key points have been created to assist the reader in determining his or her level of openness with regard to the subject matter. When reviewing the five key points, it is important to pay attention to any feelings or emotions that arise. Do any of the key points bring up feelings of anger, sadness, discomfort or frustration? Do any of the key points feel too 'close to home'? If the reader is triggered by a key point or several key points, this is an indication of an area that needs closer attention or focus. In fact, this could be an area that is barring or prohibiting him or her from meeting the right person.

For example after reading the forgiveness chapter, the reader may not see examples of anyone that he or she needs to forgive or anyone whose forgiveness he or she needs to obtain. At the same time, the key points around forgiveness may trigger feelings of anger or disgust. These feelings of anger or disgust are an indication of an unresolved issue that needs to be given further attention. Unresolved issues should be perceived as a gift. The gift is a space the reader is invited to enter. Inside this space, the reader will find the piece or pieces of their inner landscape that need to be healed. When the gift is perceived as a barrier that cannot be accessed, the reader has encountered a block. The block will remain in place until he or she is ready to embrace the healing that awaits them.

If the reader cannot resolve one key point or several key points, I suggest that they proceed to the next exercise: *A meditation to assist the journey*. A meditation to assist the journey was created to provide the reader with a space to explore the issue on a deeper level. These meditations are structured differently than standard meditations. They contain a relaxation, a focal point to connect with, questions for introspection and a declaration that is read aloud by the reader. The declaration provides the reader with an opportunity to verbally state his or her desire to change their law of attraction.

If the reader cannot resolve the issue after having done both the key points and the meditation, I suggest moving forward to the next chapter. Before moving onto the next section, the reader should return to the problem chapter in order to resume his or her work on that issue. Upon returning and reviewing the chapter a second time, the reader may have better luck. If not, I suggest that the reader continue to move forward with the intention to re-visit the issue at a future date.

There are three factors that influence the ability to resolve and make peace with an issue. They are: awareness of the issue, a willingness to work through the issue and putting oneself in a place of non-judgment as they walk through the issue. If the reader commits to the process, shifts will occur over time.

Finally, the reader should view the chapters, the key points and the meditations as steps taken along the journey. As the reader progresses through the book, he or she will begin to feel different about what they desire in a relationship. By the time the reader gets to the final chapter, he or she should be ready to begin the manifestation process.

PART I

THE ILLUSIONS OF DATING

CHAPTER 1

SOUL MATE, SOUL MATE, WHERE FOR ART THOU, SOUL MATE?

"When will I meet my soul mate?" "Where is my Romeo?" "Where is my Juliet?" "Why isn't she in my life now? I'm ready ... I'm waiting ..." "Where is he?" "Where is she? What's taking so long?"

As a psychic who specializes in helping people align with their dreams, I have heard these statements and others like them a hundred times. We are all on the lookout for the "one" who will make our life wonderful and amazing. We are all on the lookout for our Romeo or our Juliet and the pledges of love and devotion that come with finding him or her, without the tragic Shakespearean ending. We are conditioned to believe that the arrival of our soul mate will make the sky bluer, the sun brighter, and life perfect. We do not realize that this belief puts a lot of pressure on a person we haven't even met.

What is a soul mate? A soul mate is someone you've known before, loved before, suffered with and felt joy with before this lifetime. In many cases, soul mates have spent several past lives together. The past life with a soul mate may have occurred anywhere in the world, at any time. You and your soul mate may have switched genders over the lives you spent together.

When you enter a relationship with a soul mate, it is important to do so from a place of openness and love. If you agree to work through the issues and baggage you both bring, you can eventually have a wonderfully fulfilling and loving relationship with him or her. One of the most amazing things about being with a soul mate is that you'll be supported, respected, and 100-percent accepted for who you are. You may not see eye to eye or agree on everything, but you will feel your mate loving and encouraging you. The expression "the eyes are the window to the soul" is true with regard to soul mates. When you lock eyes with your soul mate for the first time in this life, you know intellectually you've never met before. However, the soul feels the familiarity.

For the past sixty years, TV and movies have programmed us to believe that there is an elusive "soul mate" who is going to make us feel complete. Our belief is that he or she is the perfect match for us — the yin to our yang, the half that will make us whole. One of my favorite movies about soul mates is the 2001 film *Serendipity*, starring John Cusack and Kate Beckinsale. The movie begins with Jonathan and Sara (Cusack and Becksinsale, respectively) reaching out to grab the same pair of black gloves in New York City's Bloomingdale's department store. After some flirtatious banter, they decide to go to a coffee shop called Serendipity to discuss who gets to keep the gloves. A short while later, they leave the coffee shop and go ice skating in Central Park. As the magical evening comes to an end, the pair decides to prompt fate to see if their paths are destined to cross again. Believing they will be reunited if it is in the stars, Sara pulls the book *Love in the Time of Cholera* from her bag and writes her phone number in it. She tells Jonathan that she'll sell the book to a random bookstore the next day. Jonathan writes his number on a five-dollar bill and hands it to Sara. She gives it to a street vendor to purchase a newspaper. As Jonathan and Sara part, the hands of destiny take over. If the fates have their way, the book will find its way to Jonathan and the five-dollar bill will return to Sara.

The story continues several years later; both Jonathan and Sara are engaged to other people. With the impending arrival of their respective wedding days, neither has been able to forget the other and the magical night they shared. Unable to move forward and ignore the past, Jonathan and Sara set out to find each other. After a number of near-miss connections, Jonathan and Sara reunite on the ice in Central Park and live "happily ever after." This delightfully funny romantic comedy makes you believe in soul mates and in the power of serendipitous events to bring us together.

While Hollywood convinces us that "happily ever after" results when you meet a soul mate, the truth is that soul mates come into our lives with unfinished baggage. In many cases, there are usually one, if not two, unresolved issues that one or both of the parties have agreed in the past to work through. While you may not remember your past actions, your soul remembers the *pain*. Meeting a soul mate can bring you the highest levels of joy but also the agony of pain. A soul mate knows you well enough to get under your skin and push your buttons. A soul mate is capable of triggering your unresolved issues so you can begin to face them. The arrival of a soul mate into our lives is a gift. When two souls reunite, they have the ability to heal old wounds and erase karma. However, free will is always a factor. Once a meeting between two souls has occurred, one or both souls may decide that they do not want to heal the wound or erase the karma.

While working in New York City several years ago, I signed up for a ballroom class at a large dance studio. I arrived early and was told to have a seat. I sat down on the couch, and while getting comfortable, gave a quick side glance to the persons on my left and right, like most New Yorkers. When I glanced to my left, I noticed a guy looking at me. I gave a quick smile and continued to look at the dance schedule I'd grabbed. I did not know that the guy on my left had a reaction when our eyes met. He recognized me from a past life and knew my soul. I, however, had no reaction and didn't recognize him at all. Did I have soul mate amnesia? No. It was more important for his growth and learning that he recognize me versus me recognizing him. A month or two later, after we'd dated a few times, he admitted the feelings he'd experienced on the couch. I smiled when he told me the story.

"We've known each other before," I said.

"Did you recognize me?" he asked.

"No, I didn't. It's okay. We're together now," I answered.

I never felt any type of recognition the entire time we dated. Why? We weren't meant to be together in this lifetime. We were meant to meet, learn from each other, and move on. Did I learn anything? Yes, lots of things. Did he? Of course! Will we be together again in another lifetime? Probably. In this incarnation, we both had different paths to follow. We had different agendas to fulfill with regard to soul growth. When I think of him now, I remember him as a wonderful teacher. I hope I was a wonderful teacher for him. I honor the lessons I learned from him. As soul mates, we had contracted to meet in this lifetime, but we hadn't contracted for forever.

Here is another example of a soul mate reconnection. The time: the 1870s; the place: the rural South. A man was in charge of a group of workers in the field. He was brash, challenging, difficult, and at times terrifying. He ruled with an iron fist; his temper was not to be crossed. His workers consisted of a group of immigrant women and men. Their language and skills were minimal, but they did what they were told. They lived in fear of this man and his fits of rage. As hard as the man tried, he could not help himself — he found that he was attracted to one of the women. She was beautiful, quiet, docile, respectful, and trembled in his presence. He was in awe of her. He found himself watching her. When he saw her, he looked for a glimpse of something in her eyes. Because of his position, the man had to be demanding and harsh. The man would have liked to put those feelings aside in order to get to know the woman. Throughout this incarnation, he received nothing from her. She was scared and nervous around him. At the end of his life, the man mourned his lost opportunity with the woman.

Shift to the twenty-first century in Southern California. A man spots a beautiful woman across a crowded dance floor. His heart stops, his breathing becomes labored, and he feels his throat tighten. *Who is she?* He asks himself. *I must meet her.* As he begins to walk in her direction, he realizes he cannot use his standard lines with her. He knows he needs to put all his phoniness aside and be real. He approaches her and asks her to dance. She accepts. While they dance, he makes small talk and attempts to be pleasant and nice. When the music ends, he walks her back to her seat. She thanks him, and he walks away.

Several months later he sees her again. Once again, he approaches her and speaks to her from a place of openness. He cannot tell whether she is interested in him or if she's being polite. Risking rejection, he asks for her phone number. Several days later, he calls her, and they begin to date. Each time he picks her up, he arrives with a red rose and behaves like a complete gentleman all evening. He is open and honest. Each evening after dropping her off, he finds himself more and more drawn to her.

She is touched by his romantic efforts, but she knows she cannot trust him. Her intuition warns her that something isn't right.

While she admits to having been struck by their initial meeting, she has had mixed feelings about getting to know him. She finds him uncommunicative, distant, and odd. Most importantly, she senses he isn't always genuine with her and that he's hiding something. The more she listens to her gut, the more she knows she cannot trust him. After some consideration and the realization that he's closed off, she breaks it off with him. He takes the breakup badly.

In this reunion of two soul mates, the man was unable to get over the infatuation he'd felt from their previous lifetime in the South. While he realized that he needed to be real in his experiences with her, he was unable to show his true self for fear of rejection. While he felt he behaved in a gentleman-like manner, she felt his actions were contrived. In many ways, he still saw himself as the master who was in charge of the workers and in charge of his emotions. He unconsciously feared showing his true self to her, believing the revelation of his true nature could prove disastrous. She, on the other hand, unconsciously remembered the distant, challenging dictator who caused her to tremble with fear. Because of the past distrust she felt for this man, she found herself unable to release it in the present.

In this situation, we see two soul mates from a past lifetime who agreed to reunite. The reunion of these two souls proved to be unfruitful because neither was ready to let go of the past and address their common underlying issue of trust. While the circumstances of their meeting in this lifetime placed them on a parallel level of power, the challenges of their past lives proved to be too difficult to master in this meeting. If their reunion had occurred when both of them were more open to working through their trust issues, the union could have served as a training ground for their souls' growth.

What's the lesson here? We need to change our perception of a "soul mate." We need to get real about the Hollywood ending and the "happily ever after" part. We may meet that special soul mate and spend time with him or her, but down the road we may marry someone else. This does not ruin the fairytale. We need to trust in what God has in store for us. We need to be open to the possibility that in this lifetime we are destined to be with the soul who will give us the highest growth potential.

Additionally, we need to trust that the soul we end up with may not be our soul mate. There's a saying: "There's our plan for our lives, and there's God's plan for our lives. God's plan *works!*" Isn't it comforting to know that we don't walk the path alone? We may think we do, but we don't. We're always receiving guidance. We only need to listen.

KEY POINTS FOR REFLECTION AND JOURNALING

1. What is your definition of a soul mate?
2. Do you feel that Hollywood has influenced your view of relationships? How?
3. Are you willing to change your idea of "happily ever after"?
4. Can you see differences between a real relationship and the fairytale relationships we see on TV and movie screens?
5. Can you let go of your attachment to finding your soul mate and be open to the right partner for you?

A MEDITATION TO ASSIST THE JOURNEY

Find a quiet spot. Take several deep breaths. Focus on the breath going in and out of the body. Let go and release. Let go and release. Let go and release. Beginning with your toes and traveling up to the top of your head, slowly take the time to relax your body. Imagine all your stresses fading and floating away. Take several more deep breaths. When you are fully relaxed, see yourself standing in the middle of a beautiful meadow. Feel your feet standing on the earth. Take a deep breath and allow yourself to send roots from the bottom of your feet into the earth. Connect with Mother Earth. As you connect with Mother Earth, look around you. See the bright blue sky, feel the warmth of the sun, smell the wildflowers and hear the birds softly chirping. Allow yourself to feel completely at peace here. Take a moment and connect with your heart. Go deep into the most beautiful cavern of your heart and allow yourself to feel the love there. What color do you see here? Is it gold? Is it green? Is it pink? Is it luminescent? Allow that love to spiral out of your heart and wash over you from head to toe. Feel this love resonating and vibrating all around you. Take several deep breaths. When you are ready state the following aloud:

'I call-in the soul who will enable me to experience deep, passionate love and achieve the best and highest growth potential for myself in this lifetime. I know and I trust that this soul is the one that has been chosen for me in this lifetime. I promise to offer this soul deep and passionate love. I promise to assist this soul in achieving their best and highest growth potential in this lifetime. I am grateful for the commitment I have made to myself as I walk this journey to the right relationship.'

When you are ready, return to the room and take notice of any sensations or feelings you are experiencing. If possible, take notes or record your impressions in a journal.

CHAPTER 2

SHE'S NOT MY TYPE ...
HE'S NICE, BUT NOT MY TYPE ...

Meredith has worked with me for several years. Her journey to find the right relationship, has been filled with detours, like that of many others. After exhausting the avenues of meeting guys through friends, the gym, and clubs, Meredith decided to try online dating. At a session, we discussed the new guy in her life.

"Sam is very sweet," Meredith told me. "I can tell he really likes me. He is attentive, calls when he's supposed to, checks in, et cetera."

"What's the problem?" I asked.

"Well, this is going to sound stupid, but he has a physical trait that doesn't fit in with my vision of an ideal mate," she replied.

"What's the trait?" I asked.

"He's got a funny nose," she said.

"A funny nose?"

"It's long and crooked on the end. His nose goes a bit to the left … It's not really that noticeable at first, unless you are looking at his face closely," she said.

"Okay. His nose isn't perfect. Is this trait tolerable to you?" I asked.

"Well, I don't know. I really wanted a guy with a perfect nose," she said.

"In other words, he doesn't match your ideal type because of his nose?" I added.

"Yes," she said.

"Well, you have two choices. Accept Sam and his less-than-perfect nose and make an attempt to get to know him better, or break it off with him and continue looking," I said.

"I don't know what to do. I don't think I can get beyond the nose," she said.

"Is this really a deal breaker for you?" I asked.

"I don't know," she said.

"It sounds like you've made your decision," I said. "You need to tell Sam as soon as possible."

"I feel bad about hurting his feelings," she said.

"Meredith, you need to tell him that you are looking for something else. Don't string him along. Do it quickly," I added.

"Well, I just wish his nose was perfect," she said.

"His nose is his nose. Call it a character flaw or a slight physical imperfection, but his nose is his nose. It sounds to me like you won't accept it," I said.

"No. I'm not sure I can," she said.

"Do the right thing and tell him that you are moving on. If you feel this way, you can't let this go on. You know that."

What exactly is "type"? In Meredith's case, her ideal partner had to have very specific physical features based on a type she'd created a long time ago. In our minds, we all carry the image of the type of person we feel is our ideal mate.

- He has to be tall, dark, and handsome.
- She's that girl-next-door type.
- She's a librarian type.
- He's the strong, silent type.

The list goes on and on. We develop our type based on the actors, actresses, musicians, idols, and influential people we see on TV and in the movies and other media we are constantly exposed to. They provide the forum within which we develop our tastes for the attractive and the unattractive. Two additional factors influence the creation of our type. The first is our peers, and the second is the dynamic we have with our parents. Because we want their approval and respect, our peers can affect our type. We pay attention to what they consider attractive or unattractive, even if it doesn't tie into what we feel is attractive or unattractive. Parental dynamics also affect our type. While we consciously try to date our type, we unconsciously draw in partners who have qualities or characteristics similar to the parent we have unfinished business with.

In many cases, our relationship to dating a specific type is unrealistic. Whether we want to admit it or not, our type was often created by the media. How many women in the 1980s watched the movie *St Elmo's Fire* and didn't want to date a rebellious Rob Lowe type? How many men in the 1990s watched *Beverly Hills 90210* and found themselves desiring a date with the sassy Jenny Garth? Actors and actresses playing roles become the ideal type of person we'd love to date and marry. In other generations, women swooned over Frank Sinatra, Elvis Presley, James Dean, and Marlon Brando. Men have swooned over Marilyn Monroe, Cheryl Tieges, Farrah Fawcett, and Pamela Anderson. Today, teens swoon over Justin Bieber in the same way women went crazy for the Beatles. Unfortunately, when we allow the media to create our ideal type, we surrender to the process of idealizing and idolizing a caricature, character, or cartoon-like model for what another human being can provide us. An actor's role is a depiction of a character, not the true essence or personality of that actor. The same is true for musicians, writers, athletes, sports figures, politicians, and reality stars. We tend to not distinguish the artist from the art. Rob Lowe has very little in common with the role he played in *St. Elmos' Fire*, and Jennie Garth is nothing like the role she played on *Beverly Hills 90210*. Confusing the actor, actress, musician, singer, or candidate with the roles they portray leads us on a journey of seeking an ideal mate who lacks true human complexities.

While doing a reading, many times I will see that a client is going to meet a potential boyfriend or girlfriend. The first question I am usually asked is, "What does he or she look like?" I indicate that she's got light hair or his eyes are dark. Then clients typically ask me, "Who does he or she look like?" because they are trying to see whether the unmet person fits their type, whether he or she matches that ideal person they've dreamed about.

Before the Internet, there was the blind date. You did not see a picture of the person in advance. You had to wait until you met the potential love interest in person. At that point, you were either thrilled or disappointed. During the blind date, you might have been filled with feelings of joy or dread as you shared a meal with the person. You prayed the evening would never end or that it would end in record time.

Today, dating websites like Match.com and E-Harmony help promote type by asking prospective candidates to include a photo or photos with their listing, allowing others to see whether a potential new mate fits their desired physical type before an introduction has occurred. Many people think that dating sites will assist them in speeding up the timetable to finding the right partner. Why? We live in a busy world; time is a valuable commodity. As a result, we want our search to be quick and easy. And we do not want to kiss a frog when we could be kissing a prince or a princess.

Have you ever gone on a date and decided he or she was nice but not your type? When you get hung up on type, you limit yourself. When you say that someone isn't your type, aren't you really saying that you weren't attracted to him? You do not take a second look at someone or give him an additional thought, dismissing him because he doesn't compare to your ideal type.

Sadly, when there is no initial spark, we close our eyes and our mind to a person. Instead of exploring what is new and taking the time to develop something with someone we don't have chemistry with, we tread the same pathways and date the same type of people over and over.

Recently a client complained to me that a guy in her office was flirting with her. Admitting that she was flattered, her next statement was that she wasn't interested.

"Why aren't you interested?" I asked

"He's nice, but not my type," she replied.

"You know that type is just hype, right?" I asked.

"Well, I really don't find him attractive," she said.

"Hmm. Is there no chemistry?" I asked.

"I don't know. I haven't tried to get to know him. He's just this funny guy I work with."

"I see the potential for more. But you need to think outside the box. Why don't you go out with him once and see what happens? Be open. Stop dating your type," I added.

She called me several weeks later to tell me that they'd gone out a few times and that she was enjoying herself. She realized that there was chemistry between them. She admitted that putting aside her type had helped her to open to him in a new way.

If we have an ideal type, why aren't we attracting them into our lives? We might meet someone who has some of the qualities of our desired type, but we need to get realistic about the fantasy. No one is perfect. The expectation that our type will solve all our problems, make us happy, take care of us, and never hurt us blocks us from seeing the human-ness of the person. One person cannot and should not meet all of our needs. Real people make choices and decisions that aren't always in alignment with their best intentions. When we make the choice to see our type as a living person with foibles and frailties, we begin to accept the same within ourselves. We need to accept the fact that no one is responsible for making us happy or hurting us or removing our loneliness.

The law of attraction says "like attracts like." We unconsciously attract those who are vibrating at the same level that we are. The law of attraction does not say "like attracts desire." In order to attract the type we desire, we need to get ourselves into the right alignment and do the necessary work on ourselves, which requires commitment, strength, and devotion. By opting to do the work, we will find ourselves in a new place and space. At that time, we will be ready for our dream relationship, because our attraction qualities will have shifted.

Sadly, many people do not want to do the work to get themselves into the right alignment. Why? The decision to do the work requires dredging up a lot of feelings that most people do not want to deal with. When we shy away from this work, we give up on our type; it becomes a distant vision we can no longer grasp. However, those who embrace the work eventually find themselves meeting and dating the right type. In essence, they are creating their own happy ending.

KEY POINTS FOR REFLECTION AND JOURNALING

1. Through what medium or media did you develop your type?
2. Do you carry an image of your type in your mind?
3. Can you see how this type limits you and holds you back?
4. Would you be willing to date someone outside of your type?
5. Are you willing to work through any issues, boundaries, and barriers you have in order to meet the right person?

A MEDITATION TO ASSIST THE JOURNEY

Find a quiet spot. Take several deep breaths. Focus on the breath going in and out of the body. Let go and release. Let go and release. Let go and release. Beginning with your toes and traveling up to the top of your head, slowly take the time to relax your body. Imagine all your stresses fading and floating away. Take several more deep breaths. When you are fully relaxed, see yourself standing in the middle of a beautiful meadow. Feel your feet standing on the earth. Take a deep breath and allow yourself to send roots from the bottom of your feet into the earth. Connect with Mother Earth. As you connect with Mother Earth, look around you. See the bright blue sky, feel the warmth of the sun, smell the wildflowers and hear the birds softly chirping. Allow yourself to feel completely at peace here. Take a moment and connect with your heart. Go deep into the most beautiful cavern of your heart and allow yourself to feel the love there. What color do you see here? Is it gold?

Is it green? Is it pink? Is it luminescent? Allow that love to spiral out of your heart and wash over you from head to toe. Feel this love resonating and vibrating all around you. Take several deep breaths. Take a moment and bring to mind your images and thoughts about 'type'. Allow these images to float in front of you. Do not judge the images. Just allow. When you are ready, places these images in a beautiful white balloon. See the images fill the balloon. When you are ready, let go of the balloon and watch it begin to climb higher and higher. As it floats away, state the following aloud:

'I release these visions of my ideal type. I let go of my attachment to type. I allow the right partner to enter my life. I choose to shift my law of attraction qualities. I am in the proper alignment. I am grateful for the commitment I have made to myself as I walk this journey to the right relationship.'

When you are ready, return to the room and take notice of any sensations or feelings you are experiencing. If possible, take notes or record your impressions in a journal.

CHAPTER 3

HIS-STORY, HER-STORY

We all have a story. How did your story begin? Where in the family order were you born: first-born, middle child, or the baby? What was the make-up of your family: how many boys? How many girls? What was your role in the family dynamic? Were you the good girl or boy or the black sheep of the family? Did you like that role? Did you dislike that role? Which parent was the disciplinarian? Which parent favored you? Which did you feel lacked affection or understanding for you? Were either of your parents too involved in your life, not involved enough, self-involved, distant or withdrawn, overbearing or protective, abusive (mentally, emotionally, physically), or an enabler who allowed the abuser to abuse?

Are your parents still married, or are you the child of divorced parents? What was your relationship with the parent who raised you versus the parent who didn't? Did one of your parents die or become very sick while you were little? If yes, how did his or her death or illness affect you? How did your parents earn a living? Did you like what they did? Did you dislike what they did? How did your parents treat money? Was it abundant? Was it scarce? How did their relationship with money affect yours? How did your parents treat birthdays and holidays? Were they good occasions filled with joy and smiles or sad days filled with dread and drama? Did your family take vacations? If so, to where? What were your vacation experiences like? Did you learn new things? Was it fun? Was it boring?

How did you get along with your siblings? How did they treat you? Did you have a favorite sibling? Did you have a sibling you didn't like? Did you have a relationship with your grandparents? What did you love about them? What did you dislike about them? What did they do for you that your parents didn't?

Did you play sports? Dance? Were your interests artistic or technical? Did you have a lot of friends or only a few? Was your family religious or was religion unimportant? How did religion shape your views? Did you like school or hate it? What was your attitude about learning? Did you have a favorite subject in school? What was it? What was your least favorite subject? Why? Do you remember what you wanted to be when you grew up? Are you living that career now?

These factors and many more comprise your "story." Your story is entirely different from anyone else's. Your story is unique to you. Your story will be different from your siblings' stories because we all perceive the world and our lives differently. Your story creates your reality: the thoughts, feelings, and expressions of your experiences. Your story directs your personality. Are you shy and socially awkward, the class clown, or comfortable with others? Are you an introvert or an extrovert? Are you a leader or a follower?

Our story is who we are, and who we are revolves around our story. Our story shapes the way we dress, the foods we eat, the clothes we wear, the things we like, the things we dislike. Our story tells us it is safe to enter a room when we hear voices or encourages us to hide when we hear yelling and screaming. Our story may make us treat everyone the same or differently. Our story may create prejudices toward a certain skin color, ethnic group, or sexual orientation. Our story may force us into a career, a marriage, or a friendship that doesn't suit us but suits our story. Our story becomes us, and we become our story.

During our youth, we accept our story wholeheartedly. We believe this is the way life is. We never question our story. Why would we? However, as we mature, we are faced with the realities of life. We see that things don't work out the way we had hoped or anticipated. We realize that the life we envisioned for ourselves doesn't always seem to be within our grasp. We wonder:

- Why we can't find the man or woman of our dreams?
- Why we can't find the ideal career?
- Why we are not successful?
- Why we are constantly drawn to meeting the same sorts of people?
- Why we can't have or earn more money?

The reason why our lives are unfulfilled is because we cling to our stories. Most people do not realize that their story is inhibiting them from reaching their desires. Most people are unaware of how their attachment to their story affects the partners they draw to themselves. Attachment to story involves subconscious and conscious thought. We are aware of the problems we were raised with (conscious thought), but often we don't see how deeply those problems affect us (subconscious thought). In many instances, our story is so embedded within us that we cannot see that it holds us back from experiencing life fully.

How does attachment to our story keep us from getting the relationship we want? Attachment to our story keeps us grasping the past, ties us to old memories and beliefs about ourselves, and enslaves us to who we aren't anymore. Combined with law of attraction–type thoughts from the past, attachment to our story stunts our growth. When we remain trapped in the old, we cannot evolve into the new. The old tapes and movies that play in our minds hinder us more than we know.

If there's a tape playing in your head that says you aren't loveable, you'll block your ability to meet the right partner until you stop listening to it. If you keep replaying the movie in which you were habitually beaten by one of your parents, you'll never find a lover who isn't abusive to you.

Take a moment and think about your life. Have you found yourself unable to make changes or shifts in your life because of your past? Are you still haunted by comments your parents made? Did they tell you that you weren't good enough or worthy enough? Are you afraid to make your own choices because you never had their guidance or support? Do you feel paralyzed? Do you find yourself in one disappointing relationship after another? Do you feel that you can't make any changes to your life without asking your parents' permission? If yes, maybe they were too involved in dictating your life. Do you know how to live autonomously?

Do you think of your relationship with one or both of your parents as difficult, challenging, or disappointing? Are you aware that you chose your parents before you came here? We all enter into a soul contract before coming to planet Earth. You may find it hard to believe, but you chose your parents. You chose them because they were able to teach you the lessons you needed to learn in this lifetime. No, you don't remember choosing your parents or the lessons you needed to learn from them, but you were a part of the process. Take a moment and think about the dynamic you have with your parents. Do you know what your parents taught you? Can you look beyond the pain, disappointment, and tears to see the gift or the teaching they gave you? What have you learned by being their son or daughter? What knowledge or message did they impart to you that you'll pass along? How will you pass that message along? When you can see the gift, you can begin to loosen the attachment. Until you do this work, you'll never see that attachment to your story keeps you *safe!* Additionally, attachment to your story gives you an excuse to blame or point fingers at your less-than-perfect parental role models. Attachment to your story means you remain contracted and small instead of expanded and full.

When I work with clients, we discuss issues involved in their story and the importance of doing the necessary work to make their lives better. The work can involve a number of different facets. However, each client's work varies according to their level of openness and their willingness to move ahead.

Our story, whatever it is (and we all have one), is *just a story*. Nothing more. Our story defines or confines us as we allow. The more work we do to release our story, the less the story impacts our relationships. Awareness is the key to understanding that unfinished parental business leads to us date the same "father figure" or "mother figure" over and over again, until we absorb the lessons we need to learn. We can break the pattern by working through our story, releasing it, and then embracing the new self that surfaces. Doing the work yields great results. We align ourselves to meet the right person.

Denise is a client who has been working with me for several years. At first glance, Denise appears to be one of those women you don't want to cross. She's tough, she's rough, and she doesn't mess around. Denise has a hard shell that masks her sadness over not knowing her real father. He disappeared when she was only an infant. For a long time, Denise struggled with the decision over whether to locate her father. Finally, she decided to hire a private investigator. He conducted a thorough search but was unable to discover an exact location where Denise's dad lived. Denise learned that her father was very good at hiding. Each time Denise felt she was getting closer, she'd encounter another roadblock. After exhausting a lot of money on three different private investigators, Denise stopped all efforts to find her dad. Denise came to the conclusion that her dad was a loser who didn't want to be found. She told me she didn't care if her father ever appeared in her life. Denise had shifted from a place of loss and sadness to a place of anger and fury, which spilled over into a tempestuous relationship Denise had with a man she'd previously had little feeling for.

Denise admits to an erratic dating history. During the course of our work together, Denise and I discussed how she felt about her father. Because of his absence, Denise suffers over issues of abandonment and self-love. Denise likes to be in control of her emotions and relationships. As a result, Denise never becomes too committed or too intense or falls too deeply for anyone. She dated and entered a long-term relationship here and there, but she never fully gave herself to anyone.

As Denise's perception of men shifted and evolved, her ability to draw in a man who resonated and vibrated at a similar dynamic multiplied. As hard as it was to admit, Denise found herself falling hard for Ryan. Because of the underlying dynamic of anger between the two of them, Denise and Ryan argued — *a lot*! She often told me the stories of minor incidents between the two of them that would blow up into huge arguments. They'd fight, argue, scream, and yell. Later they'd make up. Over time, the instability of the relationship took its toll. Six months into the relationship after a particularly challenging argument, Denise contacted me for an emergency session. Denise was raw, exhausted, and inconsolable. Half a box of tissues later, we finally got down to the meat of her issue. I explained to Denise that in the relationship with Ryan she was working through unresolved issues with her father. I asked Denise to look at the parallels between how she felt toward her dad and how she felt toward Ryan. We discussed feelings of abandonment, disappointment, lack of commitment, anger, and loss. Denise resented her dad, and she resented Ryan. I explained to Denise that Ryan had come into her life to help her heal her story.

"Why?" she asked me.

I told her the time had come for this work to be done.

"Why him?"

I told her that Spirit felt he was the right person to assist her in doing this work.

"Why now?" she asked.

"Because you need to do this work in order to be free from your story, to move forward and to have a great life."

Denise told me she loved Ryan. She admitted that they argued fervently and that he caused her a lot of pain. Despite the tumultuous nature of their relationship, Denise said she could not picture life without him. I explained that she was in the midst of "doing the work" and that her feelings about her dad and her boyfriend were comingled. I explained that in time she would achieve better clarity about what this relationship was teaching her and that someday she'd be grateful for this relationship because it would free her.

Six months later, after a lot of work on her part, Denise said good-bye Ryan. She made peace with him and also with her feelings toward her father. Today Denise is working on getting herself into alignment to meet the right man for her.

Often our story is not easy to work through, but the benefits can prove to be very transformative if we embrace the healing process. In coming to terms with our story, we need to understand our soul contract and the role it plays in our life. What is a soul contract? For a moment imagine yourself not as a human being living in a body but as a soul. You, this soul, decide to come to planet Earth because you want to advance your spiritual growth. However, before you can come to planet Earth, you must write your soul contract. You sit down with Spirit and discuss what you'd like to accomplish while on planet Earth. For example:

- You want to be a loving, supportive spouse
- You want to learn patience
- You want to be a parent
- You want to express creatively
- You want to love and experience the depths of love
- You want to help save the earth
- You want to make a difference in medicine, science, business, or teaching
- You want to understand humility
- You want to increase your ability to be selfless

The list goes on and on. During your discussions, you decide on the parents who'll raise you, the circumstances and the issues that you'll experience with your parents, the country you'll grow up in, and the language you'll speak. You'll also pick the people you'll have as boyfriends or girlfriends, the lovers that you've been with in other lifetimes that you'll meet, and the children you'll bear. You'll choose the vocation(s) you'll perform, the karma that needs to be worked through, the experiences you need to have, and the way you'll leave the world when all of your tasks and lessons have been fulfilled. You will be assigned a team of angels and spirit guides to be available and assist you in your journey. When the contract negotiations are over and the contract has been agreed to and signed by all parties and everyone has shaken hands, you'll leave to go to planet Earth. When you arrive on planet Earth, you *forget* all about your contract. You won't remember anyone you are supposed to meet, know what you are here to do, or be aware of your lessons and teaching. Why? If you remembered your contract, you wouldn't have a full human experience. You need to forget all you agreed to and be open to your soul's journey. Spirit will watch over you and give you subtle guidance if you start to veer off track. Forgetting is critical to making sure you have the experiences you agreed to. If you knew in advance the guy or girl to avoid so you wouldn't have your heart broken, you'd never experience that teaching, and you need that teaching for your soul's growth. Additionally, if you knew that the car accident you'd get into at age twenty-one was going to happen, you'd never learn to drive or you'd move to New York City, where no one drives. The car accident was meant to teach you a strong lesson about humility.

We all have a unique contract that we've come here to fulfill. Meeting our contractual obligations seems easy while we're on the other side, but it proves challenging once we are in physical form. Often, clients will say that life is hard, at times too much to deal with. Our biggest challenges come in relationships. Many people have a hard time accepting that a love relationship isn't meant to be. In some cases, two souls that have been together in past incarnations will agree to meet again but not be together in this incarnation. In reality, you may be meant to spend the rest of your life with someone else. A lot of the time it has to do with the fact that each soul is striving for different levels of growth this time around. Having faith in your soul contract allows you to recognize that the person you are destined to be with in this lifetime will assist your soul in reaching its highest level for this incarnation.

Back when I was living on the East Coast, I met a man I knew I'd known before in a past life. He had some spiritual beliefs and didn't realize we had known each other before until we'd dated a few times. Finally he realized that he had been my brother back in ancient Pompeii. He also knew that we'd both died trying to escape the volcanic explosion. In this lifetime we'd agreed to meet again, to date and get to know each other, but we had very different agendas. He was destined to marry another woman and spend his life dealing with panic attacks (a carryover from our sudden deaths in Pompeii). I, on the other hand, was meant to reconnect him with concepts like reincarnation, karma, and the power of a divine connection. I was also destined to leave the East Coast and live my life in Southern California. While we were only in each other's lives for a brief period of time this time, the importance of our meeting was karmic. When we parted ways, we both understood that we had gotten what we needed from each other and were moving on to fulfill our pathways.

Examples of other contractual issues include clients who are straddled with debt, have had multiple marriages or lovers, are very career-oriented and prefer success and fame to family and partnership, etc. The important thing to acknowledge is that the person who is saddled with debt chose that experience in order to learn something. The same is true for someone who has been married multiple times or someone who chooses career over family. Most people aren't sure why they have come to the earth. They know that they are here. Being here and living here is not by chance. You come here by *choice*! If you aren't sure why you are here, think about what your "bliss" is. What is the one thing that makes your soul soar?

I had a client whose greatest desire was motherhood. From the time she was a young girl, all she ever wanted was to be a mother. However, she was the product of divorced parents. Her father had cheated on her mother many times. Her parents eventually divorced. Her father remarried; he cheated several times on his second wife during the course of my client's upbringing. My client knew she had trust issues. Together, we worked through layer after layer of her trust issues, our goal forgiveness and release. In time, she forgave her father, released the hate she'd carried for him, reevaluated her relationship with her mother, found comfort in the beginnings of trust, and eventually married a wonderful man. One year later, when she found out she was pregnant, she felt ready to realize her dream of finally becoming a mom.

You may not remember why you are here, but you are here because your soul chose to come here to grow. You made a contract. My soul contract involves doing readings, teaching, conducting healing sessions, and sharing my wisdom through writing. I am honored to do the work I'm here to do. Each session with a client provides me with a level of satisfaction I cannot describe. I am fulfilled.

Every day Spirit gifts us with choices, opportunities, and experiences to help us meet our contractual terms. The decision to fully live our contract lies with us. When our time here is finished, we'll sit down once again as a soul and have a meeting with our team. We'll review what we accomplished, what we failed at, and our overall human experience. Everything we face here has to do with our soul's growth.

A big portion of our soul contract has to do with karma. What is karma? I'm sure we've all seen or heard variations of the following statements:

It's her karma.
Oh, well, I guess he's got bad karma.
You shouldn't do that. It's bad karma.

Karma is defined, "As you sow, so also shall you reap." The seeds that you sow, the thoughts that you have, the words that you speak, the actions that you take, so shall you reap (receive) in return. I think of karma as cause and effect. If your actions are good and God-like, then good things will come to you. If your actions are bad and un-God-like, then bad or negative things will come to you. Here's an example.

Several years ago I had a client who was in the music business. He was so focused on the career of one of his peers that he lost focus on his own career. He envied the accomplishments of his peer. He wanted everything that that person had worked hard for. Instead of wishing that person well and congratulating him for his success, he bad-mouthed him and gossiped about him every opportunity he got. He loved to tell people that the person lacked talent and how terrible an artist he was. He expended a lot of negative energy and negative karma in putting that person down, criticizing and mocking him. In effect, his actions were sabotaging his career, but he couldn't see that. He couldn't see that his career was going nowhere. If he had focused on his own path, his own goals, his own desires, and his own aspirations, he would have recognized that his path was different. He would have seen that his own success would find its way to him in the right time. He was also unable to understand the law of attraction and how his ongoing negativity only brought more negativity to him. Working with this client, I enabled him to see how his actions were hurting him, and only him. Today he's switched his focus to his own career, and he's on his way to his own success.

There is a misconception that karma is a bad thing. Karma can only be considered a bad thing if we perceive it that way. Perceiving karma is similar to how we view the glass: half full? Half empty? Karma heals, but we have to embrace the healing instead of fight it. Through karma, we are able to learn lessons and grow on a soul level. While I agree that karmic lessons are not easy, they do help us achieve the growth we've set out for. Haven't some of the hardest lessons we've learned come out of difficult times? Can any of us say that we learned a major soul lesson through an experience that was easy? I doubt it.

I see karma arise noticeably in romantic relationships. Most people are surprised to learn that a relationship that ended due to jealousy, infidelity, or violence had major karmic issues and ties. You may have been the one who was left by your husband in this lifetime, but perhaps the last time around you left him. If you are victimized by a lover, you may have been the victimizer the last time around. Maybe you abandoned your lover in this lifetime because the last time around he abandoned you. Karmic ties run very deep and can be very painful. Karma also has the ability to help us work out control issues and power issues.

If life is our classroom, then we are learning, growing, and evolving all the time. Each time we incarnate here, karma is a valuable tool in helping us further our life education. Having a grasp of our story and its effects on our thoughts and behavior, as well as understanding our soul contract and the role of karma in our lives, gives us knowledge. Knowledge is vital in enabling us to make the right decisions about who we date, who we enter into relationships with, and ultimately who we choose to commit to.

KEY POINTS FOR REFLECTION AND JOURNALING

1. Do you understand the components of your story?
2. Are you clear about the challenges your story has presented to you?
3. Reflect on key experiences in your life. Can you see your story at work?
4. Can you understand the concepts regarding soul contracts and karma? How do they shape your experience?
5. Do you embrace your experiences as gifts from Spirit or problems that need to be dealt with?

A MEDITATION TO ASSIST THE JOURNEY

Find a quiet spot. Take several deep breaths. Focus on the breath going in and out of the body. Let go and release. Let go and release. Let go and release. Beginning with your toes and traveling up to the top of your head, slowly take the time to relax your body. Imagine all your stresses fading and floating away. Take several more deep breaths. When you are fully relaxed, see yourself sitting in the middle of a beautiful meadow. Take another breath and allow yourself to go into a deeper place of relaxation. Just be. When you are ready, look around you. See the bright blue sky, feel the warmth of the sun, smell the wildflowers and hear the birds softly chirping. Allow yourself to feel completely at peace here. Take a moment and connect with your heart. Go deep into the most beautiful cavern of your heart and allow yourself to feel the love there. What color do you see here? Is it gold? Is it green? Is it pink? Is it luminescent? Allow that love to spiral out of your heart and wash over you from head to toe. Feel this love resonating and vibrating all around you. Take several deep breaths. When you are ready, allow your story and its images to pass through your mind. Allow yourself to experience the joy, the sorrow, the anger, the frustration, the confusion, the beauty, the loss, the pain, and the happiness. Be with any feelings that arise. How has your story has defined you? How have you defined your story to others? Take a few moments to focus on karma. Can you see the seeds you have sown? What have you or others reaped from the seeds you've sown? Are you willing to take ownership of your role in these actions? When you are ready state the following aloud:

'I see my story and the ways in which it has kept me safe. I see the ways in which my story defines me. I see the karma I have created. I see the words I have spoken, the thoughts I have had and how they have a cause and effect in the world. Today, I define myself in a new way. I am not my story. I am not my story. I am not my story. I am conscious of my words and thoughts. I do not create karma. I transform my energies. I shift my law of attraction qualities. I am in the proper alignment. I am grateful for the commitment I have made to myself as I walk this journey to the right relationship.'

When you are ready, return to the room and take notice of any sensations or feelings you are experiencing. If possible, take notes or record your impressions in a journal.

CHAPTER 4

THE DATING MERRY-GO-ROUND

When I was a little girl, we'd travel to the Jersey shore to walk along the boardwalk, lie in the sun, and eat a fish dinner. For my sister and I, a visit to the boardwalk was always filled with excitement and fun. I have fond memories of roller coasters, haunted houses, and the merry-go-round ride I'd always take. The merry-go-round seemed so magical to me, something out of another period in time: the beautiful carnival music, the amazing architecture, the lights that blinked and changed color, and of course the beautiful horses that slowly swayed up and down. My sister and I would wait in line, brimming with anticipation. When the moment arrived and the gate opened, we'd charge the ticket taker, jump on the merry-go-round platform, and race to the mares we'd been watching. We'd quickly decide between the brown horse, the black one, or the white one. We'd examine the ornate and jeweled saddle and figure out if our mare was dressed for battle or for fun. We'd observe our horse's expression. Was it angry, complacent, or joyful? Once in the saddle, we'd hold on tight to the gold pole and wait for the music to begin. In each and every experience, the ride was always worth the wait.

What is it about the merry-go-round that captivates us? Studies have shown that the combination of the lights, the music, and the movement evoke feelings of serenity, enjoyment, and enchantment. The feelings sparked by the merry-go-round are similar in many ways to the early stages of dating and relationships. All relationships feel special, amazing, and joyous in the beginning. All new relationships fill us with the anticipation of joy, beauty, and possibility.

While the initial stages of dating can be euphoric and magical, the realities of accepting a new love and his or her faults stare us in the face once the ride is over and the carnival music has ended. We swing from euphoric high to devastated low too quickly. In our endless search for the highs of love, we find ourselves going from lover to lover, from horse to horse. As a society, we have become bipolar in regards to relationships. We want the fun, the romance, and the magic but not the work that is involved in making a relationship last. In fact, most people admit that they lose interest in a relationship at that critical time when issues arise and need to be addressed. For many people it is easier to jump off one horse and onto another. We fail to see that while each new horse is gallant, beautiful, and evocative, they are all truly the same underneath all that dressing. One horse may be flashier than another or have a stern demeanor versus a relaxed demeanor, but the inner qualities remain the same. This holds true for the partners we date.

At first, a new partner often appears different from previous lovers. However, as the romance phase of a relationship ends, we see the same qualities emerge that we recognize from a previous partner. We see that the cycle has repeated itself again. This repetitive cycle wears us down over time. We will often ride the same merry-go-round for years until we realize we are stuck on the ride and can't get off. Why are we stuck? Why can't we jump off? We are stuck because we cannot see the law of attraction at work. The law of attraction says, "Like attracts like." We attract the partner(s) who resonate closely with the thoughts and feelings we have about ourselves. We are not usually aware of these thoughts, and we are not usually aware of what a relationship means to us. Is the relationship for companionship? Is it for sex? Is it for love? Is it for someone to take care of us? We all enter into relationships with different agendas. However, what we bring into a relationship is what we will get back. If we feel unworthy of a good, loving relationship, we will never find it until we heal those feelings of unworthiness. Until then, we are unable to recognize how we repeatedly draw the same type of partner; i.e., the man or woman who will continue to make us feel unworthy or treat us so badly that we cry out in frustration. In essence, we get what we believe we deserve. But remember — because the law of attraction is shaped by our thoughts, perceptions, and feelings, by shifting our unconscious behavior we can change the way we vibrate, the way we attract others.

In the struggle to get off the merry-go-round, we are faced with two issues. First, human beings do not like change. In fact, we enjoy embracing what is familiar and comfortable. If a man is used to dating needy women, he might be thrown off-center when encountering a woman who isn't needy at all. While he dislikes the neediness and cringes at all the drama that comes with it, he knows that this is familiar, safe ground that he has previously walked upon. This man knows how to deal with and tolerate neediness. He also knows that the neediness can be taken only for so long. At some point, the neediness becomes unbearable. He reaches his breaking point. Frustrated and disgusted, he'll walk away from the relationship. There is a fine line between truly wanting to date the unfamiliar and letting go of the familiar.

The realization that something needs to change in your thought processes means you have been stuck. Having the strength to make changes to your life takes a firm commitment.

I worked at Starbucks several years ago, and a customer asked me on a date. I agreed. We went to dinner and afterwards took a drive in his old-fashioned car. For me, the evening was fun, relaxing, and enjoyable; however, I sensed his nervousness all night. At the end of the evening, he offered to walk me to my apartment. When we approached my door, he admitted his nervousness. When I asked him why he'd been nervous, he revealed that I was different from the women he was used to dating. I asked him how I was different. He told me that he always dated women with an attitude who were pretentious, high-maintenance, and could be bitchy. He said he'd felt off-balance all night because I had none of those qualities. He added that he was unsure of how to act or behave around me. I thanked him for his honesty, told him I'd enjoyed our date, and added that I'd leave it to him to decide whether he'd like to go out again or not.

It was obvious to me that our initial meeting and our subsequent date were no coincidence. Sadly, this man was unable to see that Spirit was providing him with an opportunity to get off the merry-go-round. I had been brought into his life to give him a chance to have a new and different type of dating experience. In his case, he wasn't ready to embrace the unfamiliar. I didn't hear from him for a long time after that night. I figured he'd decided to stay on his merry-go-round. Several months later, he called me.

Interestingly, I had just moved to a new location, which put an hour's driving distance between us. We never did have that second date.

The second issue we face in getting off the merry-go-round has to do with dating a partner who reminds us of familial patterns. A man who was raised by a less family-oriented mother who focused on her career would probably reject a partner with similar career aspirations. Why? In many cases, the man will feel like this potential partner's career is more important than he is. In his reality, dating a woman who has these qualities means his needs aren't a priority. A decision to date this type of woman would serve as a painful reminder of his upbringing — an upbringing he hasn't made peace with. This man may choose to date women who aren't career-oriented or are less centered on a job because it makes him more comfortable.

Similarly, a woman may shy away from a man who is a workaholic because this trait reminds her of her dad's absenteeism and distance as a father. She may opt to date a man who has very little career focus and aspiration because his ability to be more present would provide her with comfort. In both these cases, a decision to get off the merry-go-round and embrace a new type of partner would lead to new dating experiences.

I have a client, Jenna, who continually dates bad boys. She goes from one bad-boy situation to another, following the same pattern. In the beginning, Jenna is convinced that this bad boy is different from any of the others she has met. She'll brag that he is more respectful, more attentive, and more present than the previous one. Eventually, Jenna catches the bad boy cheating or in a compromising situation, and her heart gets broken. She breaks off the relationship, waits for a while, and then finds another bad boy. The cycle repeated itself. In my work with Jenna, we talked about her love/

hate dynamic with bad boys. We discussed what she found attractive about them, what they provided her, etc. Additionally, I asked Jenna to tell me about her dad. This first word out of her mouth was "*Boring!*" When I asked Jenna why her dad was boring, she explained that her dad was very stable, had a good, solid career, had provided for his family during her formative years, had put her through school and taken care of her. I asked her what was wrong with her father and added that he appeared to be a good man. Jenna explained that in her mind she saw her dad as boring. She told me that he didn't have any vices except to watch some sports on TV. She added that he liked to cook, he drank socially, he didn't smoke, he ran one to two miles a few times a week, and he enjoyed being outdoors. Again, I asked Jenna what was the problem with her dad. She finally admitted that she couldn't picture herself dating boring men like her dad, so she choose bad-boy types because they provided a lot of excitement.

Sadly, Jenna could not see that she was stuck in a cycle in which she embraced bad boys as a way of rebelling against the stability and structure a real man could bring into her life. Until Jenna could see that dating bad boys would provide no joy to her, she'd be caught up in the cycle and stuck on her merry-go-round. My work with Jenna focused on shifting her thoughts so she could embrace the positive aspects of her father figure. Additionally, I wanted her to see that the things she loathed — the stability, not having a vice, the ability to take care of his family, and a solid career — were attributes of a mature man who could be an equal in a relationship. I drew comparisons to the immature bad-boy types who were ill-prepared for dating Jenna. So far, Jenna remains on the bad-boy merry-go-round. My work with her continues.

We are never stuck on the merry-go-round. We always have a choice. We can stay on the merry-go-round and be safe, or we can get off the ride, do the work, and embrace what is unknown.

KEY POINTS FOR REFLECTION AND JOURNALING

1. How do you feel about a new love interest in the early stages?
2. Do you allow yourself to get caught up in the euphoric and magical aspects of dating? What happens when that wears off?
3. What quality or qualities do you see as repeating patterns in your dating merry-go-round?
4. Are you ready and willing to get off the merry-go-round and embrace new relationships?
5. Can you see the familial pattern(s) playing out in your merry-go-round ride? What do you want to do about it?

A MEDITATION TO ASSIST THE JOURNEY

Find a quiet spot. Take several deep breaths. Focus on the breath going in and out of the body. Let go and release. Let go and release. Let go and release. Beginning with your toes and traveling up to the top of your head, slowly take the time to relax your body. Imagine all your stresses fading and floating away. Take several more deep breaths. When you are fully relaxed, see yourself sitting in the middle of a beautiful meadow. Take another breath and allow yourself to go into a deeper place of relaxation. Just be. When you are ready, look around you. See the bright blue sky, feel the warmth of the sun, smell the wildflowers and hear the birds softly chirping. Allow yourself to feel completely at peace here. Take a moment and connect with your heart. Go deep into the most beautiful cavern of your heart and allow yourself to feel the love there. What color do you see here? Is it gold? Is it green? Is it pink? Is it luminescent? Allow that love to spiral out of your heart and wash over you from head to toe. Feel this love resonating and vibrating all around you. Take several deep breaths. When you are ready, see yourself on the dating merry-go-round. What do you like about these visions? What do you dislike about these visions? Are you ready to get off this merry-go-round? If yes, state the following aloud:

'I quit the dating merry-go-round. I see that my choice to stay on this ride has kept me safe. I reclaim the relationship of my dreams. I transform my energies. I shift my law of attraction qualities. I am in the proper alignment. I am grateful for the commitment I have made to myself as I walk this journey to the right relationship.'

When you are ready, return to the room and take notice of any sensations or feelings you are experiencing. If possible, take notes or record your impressions in a journal.

PART II:

YOUR INNER WORK: GETTING TO THE REAL YOU

CHAPTER 5

YOUR CHEATIN' HEART

When it comes to cheating, those of us who experience it fall into one of two categories: the cheater or the one cheated on. I do not know anyone who has fallen into both categories, though it is possible. The Bible says, "Thou shall not covet thy neighbor's wife." According to this ancient text, it would appear that cheating is limited to married couples. However, in today's society it is well understood that cheating is taboo whether two people are married, unmarried, dating, or living together. If cheating is morally wrong, why do so many people cheat? Why do we accept cheating as commonplace and ordinary if it is wrong and immoral? What is it that makes a person cheat? Is it because today's level of commitment is not taken seriously? Is it because we ignore or disrespect the rules that society has created regarding relationships and marriage? Do people cheat because they know they can get away with it? Do people cheat because they want to get caught?

Do people cheat because they are hoping to intentionally hurt the person they are cheating on? Is cheating done from a place of ego? Selfishness? Disrespect? Unconsciousness? Have we become a society that has ADD when it comes to monogamy? Unfortunately, it appears as though a lot of cheating is done from a place of unconsciousness.

We live in a society that promotes quick gratification over careful consideration of one's actions. During the many years I have done readings, I've always been fascinated when the topic of cheating arises. In reviewing conversations with clients, it appears to me as though cheating occurs with little or no thought as to how this action affects others. The focus is typically on filling immediate needs. These needs could include a desire for love, a desire to feel better about one's self, a desire to feel wanted and needed, or a desire to be sexually desirable to others. The focus is never about how these actions will ultimately betray trust and commitment.

Despite the consciousness-shift promised at the end of 2012, we have not opened our eyes to the karmic implications of cheating. The law of karma dictates that as you sow, so shall you reap. When one party in a relationship cheats on the other, the party who cheats sets themselves up for karmic retribution in the form of being cheated on in this or another lifetime. Additionally, a karmic debt is incurred that will remain until it is satisfied and erased. This karmic debt can carry over through several lifetimes. Belief in the existence of karma is not necessary. Karma exists for everyone. We can dismiss karma as some new-age belief or hype. We can dismiss karma as a concept that only yogis believe in. We cannot, whatever our beliefs, be excused from its laws or actions.

Movies, TV, and literature are filled with stories about cheating. The classic story about cheating is *The Scarlet Letter*. Set in seventeenth-century Boston, an ultra-conservative city, the main character of the story is Hester Prynne. As the story begins, the reader learns that Hester has been separated from her husband for two years, and while such a separation may seem common today, the reader also learns that Hester is pregnant. Because the baby cannot be her husband's, a scandal results. After the situation is brought to the attention of the town's magistrates, they proclaim Hester's actions to be unforgivable and decree that Hester wear a scarlet-colored *A* on her bodice to show everyone that Hester is an adulterer. The story details Hester's struggle and her refusal to say the name of the man who got her pregnant. While Hester never reveals her secret, the reader is told the truth.

The theme of this book centers on issues of integrity and honesty. Hester's challenge is to maintain her own level of integrity despite the actions, influences, and behaviors of others. Why did Hester keep her silence? She maintained her secret to spare of her lover and her child.

Hester's behavior may seem out of line with a modern approach to cheating, but it happened in a time when cheating was considered rare and unusual. If Hester were a celebrity or public figure in today's society, her story would be front and center on the World Wide Web for one or two days. Afterward, any follow-up news would be relegated to small captions at the bottom of the daily newspaper. Unlike seventeenth-century Boston, our modern society barely blinks over any type of cheating scandal.

In recent years, public figures, such as former president Bill Clinton and Governor Mark Sanford of South Carolina, incurred karma by their actions. The difference between them and the rest of us is that their actions fell under media scrutiny. The media had a field day covering the whys and what ifs of the Sanford scandal. These are the details.

- On June 18, 2009, Governor Sanford took a state vehicle, a Suburban, and left the governor's mansion.
- On June 18, 2009, a cell tower in the Atlanta area picked up his cell phone signal. Afterward the cell phone appears to have been turned off.
- On June 19, South Carolina law enforcement attempted to contact the governor via phone calls and texts but received no response.
- On June 20, the governor's office issued a statement indicating there was no reason for concern.
- On June 21, it became apparent that the previous day's statement was a lie because the whereabouts of the governor were completely unknown.
- On June 22, the governor's staff indicated that they'd had no communication with him in four days. The governor's wife said that she was not worried. His staff explained that the governor was hiking the Appalachian Trail.
- On June 23, the governor's wife admitted that she had not heard from her husband and that she was focused on being a mom to her children. The governor's Suburban was found at the airport. His staff stood by its previous report that he was hiking in the Appalachians.
- On June 24, Governor Sanford flew from Buenos Aires to the Atlanta airport. In an interview, the governor indicated that he'd changed his mind about hiking and wanted to do something different. Several hours later, the governor admitted to an affair with a friend from Argentina. He also admitted that the affair began one year earlier and that he went to Argentina to end the affair. Through interviews, we learn that Jenny Sanford, the governor's wife, asked her husband to leave their home two weeks prior to his mysterious disappearance.

- While major public pressure rained down upon Mark Sanford, he did not resign from office.
- Several months later, Jenny Sanford divorced her husband.
- Recently, Mark Sanford claimed Maria Belen Chapur as his soul mate. The two are still together.

Was Governor Sanford driven to cheat on his wife because of his feelings for his soul mate? Did his past life and connection with Ms. Chapur push him to behave the way that he did? Why was Governor Sanford willing to throw away his career, his marriage, and his relationship with his children in order to be with his soul mate?

HOW HAS CHEATING AFFECTED YOU?

If you are someone who has cheated, ask yourself the following questions:

1. What were the circumstances that led to cheating?
2. Do you recall what need(s) were missing in your central relationship?
3. What did you receive from cheating? Was that need fulfilled?
4. Was cheating worth it?
5. Would you cheat again?
6. How do you feel about what you did?
7. Do you wish to be forgiven?
8. Can you forgive yourself?
9. What would you change about the experience, if you did it again?
10. What would you change about yourself?

If you have been cheated on, ask yourself the following questions:

1. Did you feel something was missing in the relationship prior to the cheating?
2. Was the absence always there? If not, what brought it on?
3. Did you have a need that you felt was unmet in the relationship?
4. What was the need? Why do you feel that your need wasn't satisfied?
5. Are you glad you learned about the cheating?
6. Would you have preferred to never find out about the cheating?
7. If yes, how would not knowing have changed anything?
8. Have you forgiven this person? If not, why?
9. If you have forgiven this person, have you moved on? Have you released them from your life? If not, why?
10. Do you believe in the expressions "a cheater always cheats" or "a leopard never changes its spots"? What do these expressions mean to you?

Is there regret? Does a cheater seek forgiveness? If the cheater gets forgiveness, does this mean the slate is wiped clean and the karma eradicated? What about the person who has been cheated on? Can he or she learn to trust again? Can he or she learn to love again?

When I was in college, a guy I was dating decided to go on spring break with his friends. Spring break in Daytona, Florida, has always been known for drinking, drugs, and wild partying. I was not excited at the prospect of having my boyfriend hanging out and participating in that environment. I knew it spelled trouble. When the day came for my boyfriend to leave for his trip, he was excited, and I was anxious. When his expected return date came and passed without a word, I knew something was wrong. I became more concerned when I began sensing the energies of another woman around me. Who was she? Why was her energy around me? A few days later when my boyfriend finally surfaced, I asked him if he had cheated on me. He told me no. I didn't believe him. This exchange between us continued for several days. Each time I asked, I received the same reply. Despite my boyfriend's repeated denials, I could not ignore what I'd been seeing and sensing — the presence of a blond woman. Unable to get the truth, I stopped taking my boyfriend's phone calls. Desperate to get in touch with me, my boyfriend showed up at my house. I told him I wasn't comfortable around him anymore and that I no longer trusted him. During the course of this conversation, my boyfriend finally admitted to cheating on me. On the second day of his trip, he was drunk and had been partying for many hours on the beach, he explained. He admitted that he started chatting with a blond woman who'd been flirting with him. When they'd begun fooling around, he was torn between his feelings for me and the arousal he felt from being drunk. After being intimate with the woman, he knew he'd made a serious mistake.

His admission confirmed what I'd known all along. He had cheated on me. I knew I'd never be able to trust my boyfriend again. I chose to end the relationship. At that point, I made it clear to my boyfriend that he was not to contact me again. My boyfriend apologized to me, but the apology and the broken trust could not be remedied by the words "I'm sorry." We parted ways. I was left wondering about his ability to easily set aside our relationship to have sex with a stranger, even if he'd been drunk. Did he ever regret his behavior? I do not know. Was my ability to trust hampered by this experience? Yes, but in time I learned to forgive and release the situation.

If someone cheats once, are they always a cheater? I think cheaters will continue to behave the way they've done, until karma sets in. At that point, the experience begins to become unpleasant. The shoe is now on the other foot, and the feeling isn't comfortable. What is the purpose of cheating? Does being cheated on serve to open our eyes and make us aware that not everyone can be trusted? Do we have to lose our innocence this way? Do we have to have cheating experiences to enable us to understand the foibles of human nature? Does being cheated on make you more sensitive to it happening again? Over time, do we develop a radar for potential cheaters? While cheating breaks hearts and breaks up families, it can be avoided if we become more conscious of our behavior and our actions. At the same time, embracing consciousness comes with the responsibility to treat others with an open heart instead of a closed one.

KEY POINTS FOR REFLECTION AND JOURNALING

1. How do you perceive cheating now versus before reading this chapter?
2. How has being the cheater made you safe in relationships?
3. How has being cheated on enabled you to be a victim?
4. What is your opinion of the media's portrayal of cheating?
5. Are you willing to make peace with being a cheater or with having been cheated on? What does making peace with this behavior mean to you?

A MEDITATION TO ASSIST THE JOURNEY

This meditation can be used if someone cheated you on or if you were the one who cheated. Before beginning this meditation, please have paper and a pen ready.

Find a quiet spot. Take several deep breaths. Focus on the breath going in and out of the body. Let go and release. Let go and release. Let go and release. Beginning with your toes and traveling up to the top of your head, slowly take the time to relax your body. Imagine all your stresses fading and floating away. Take several more deep breaths. When you are ready, bring your attention to your heart. Go deep into the most beautiful cavern of your heart and allow yourself to feel the love there. What color do you see here? Is it gold? Is it green? Is it pink? Is it luminescent? Allow that love to spiral out of your heart and wash over you from head to toe. Feel this love resonating and vibrating all around you. Take several deep breaths. Bring to mind the person who hurt you or the person you hurt. Be with a vision of this person. Allow any thoughts or feelings to come to the surface. If you find yourself getting angry or emotional, take a few deep breaths and give yourself space to be with these feelings. When you are ready, begin composing a letter to this person. You will not be sending this letter to them. The purpose of this exercise is to facilitate the processing of any unresolved feelings. The letter may start in a place of anger and then progress into feelings of sorrow. The letter may start in a place of sadness, progress into feelings of liberation and then grow to anger. Allow the letter to take on a life of its own. Continue writing until the process feels finished. Please remember the following when writing the letter. Write a page and flip it over. Do not go back and re-read it.

Be true to all the emotions that come to the surface. You might find yourself brimming with anger one minute and then wallowing in tears the next. You might find yourself longing for this person or wishing that some type of harm came to them. Do not judge the feelings. They are energy. Give the experience your full attention. In order to do so, turn off your cell phone. I'd also recommend that you write with pen and paper. I do not feel this exercise is as effective when typing on a keyboard. When the letter is complete, tear it up, shred it or burn it. Again, please do not go back and re-read it. The process of re-reading it brings the energy back into you. This defeats the purpose of having released it. As you destroy the letter, state the following aloud:

'I am closing the door on this cheating experience for once and for all. I forgive myself and I forgive all the parties who were involved in this experience. I have been stuck in the past. Today, I step into a new future for myself. I reclaim the relationship of my dreams. I transform my energies. I shift my law of attraction qualities. I am in the proper alignment. I am grateful for the commitment I have made to myself as I walk this journey to the right relationship.'

When you are ready, return to the room and take notice of any sensations or feelings you are experiencing. If possible, take notes or record your impressions in a journal.

CHAPTER 6

AS WE FORGIVE THOSE WHO
TRESPASS AGAINST US

And forgive us our trespasses, as we forgive those who trespass
against us.

- The Lord's Prayer

Is there someone you need to forgive? Is it the mother who didn't
nurture you? The father who was absent? The boyfriend or girlfriend
who cheated on you? Is it the friend who said hurtful things to you
or the boss who constantly berated you? Is it the woman who hit
your car or the guy who ran over your puppy? Is it the neighborhood
kid who broke your lawn mower or the coworker who stole your
bright idea for the marketing campaign? Is it the burglar who broke
into your house or the rapist who victimized you? Is it the man or

woman who broke your heart or the child who refuses to respect you?

Ironically, when we recite the Lord's Prayer, we ask Spirit to forgive us our "trespasses," but we resist the notion of forgiving others for their trespasses. What is that unwillingness, that unrelenting feeling that we cannot forgive someone for their actions, based on? Don Luiz Miguel's *The Four Agreements* introduces the concept of separate realities. We all live in our own realities that are shaped and formed by the way we perceive the world and are created by many factors: our environment, our parents, our siblings, the country where we live, the language we speak, the climate, the customs and traditions we were raised with, our spiritual beliefs, etc. My reality is different from your reality. Your reality is different from your spouse's reality. Your spouse's reality is different from all his or her coworkers' realities. Siblings have different realities, even if they were raised by the same parents. If we all have different realities and different ways of perceiving this world we live in, isn't it easy to see how one person's actions and behaviors can be hurtful to another? The reality of someone who hits your puppy with his car and takes off is very different from the reality of someone who tried to mother you but gave you no nurturing at all. The reality of the lover who cheats on you is different from the reality of your own son or daughter disrespecting you. While we can understand and accept that a person's reality causes him or her to act a certain way, can we forgive that person for those actions?

Most people are unaware that their inability to forgive the parent who was absent, didn't nurture them, or was an alcoholic affects their ability to have good romantic relationships. In 2002, I had a client who hated his father. His disgust, disrespect, and hate for his father energetically reverberated from him. It spilled into his conversations and literally crippled his ability to move forward in life. My client came from "old money." After a nasty divorce, my client's father had shipped him off to boarding school. My client was young when that happened, and he rebelled in many ways. My client's father drank, and while my client resented his father's drinking, he began to drink as well. In the beginning, he was a social drinker, but then his drinking became more commonplace. He also turned to drugs. He got poor grades in school and acted up in any way possible. My client did all of these things to get back at his father for abandoning him and making him feel unloved and unworthy. Underneath his seething anger, my client was in a lot of pain.

As he matured, he dated many women. My client was mean to the women he dated. In time, my client felt a lot of guilt about the string of broken relationships he'd had. In each case, he abandoned his lover in the same way he felt his father had abandoned him. Although my client was aware of his pattern, he seemed unwilling to break it.

In recent years, scientific studies have proven that unresolved emotional issues manifest in the body as disease. When I met my client he was in his thirties and living in New York City. After years of harboring such a tremendous amount of anger toward his father, my client's emotions began to show up in his physical body. While doing the reading and scanning his energy fields, I told my client that he needed to get to a doctor. I could feel that he was a diabetic. His body felt thirsty to me, and I could tell he drank lots of water throughout the day. I explained to my client that diabetes is a disease of anger and frustration. I discussed with my client the fact that this illness was the result of repressed emotions that he needed to address immediately. I told my client that I could feel his pain. I added that Spirit had provided him the right soul and the right father to learn the lessons that he needed to learn in this lifetime. I explained that everything was in accordance with his soul contract. Additionally, I explained to my client the importance of forgiving his father and releasing him so that he could obtain better health and a calmer state of mind. I added that by doing the forgiveness and release work, he'd be able to attract the right type of partner, and I said that a lack of forgiveness would only make the situation grow worse. My client argued fervently with me about this. I could feel that his pain ran very deep and that all the emotions surrounding this pain prevented him from moving toward forgiveness. I also explained to him that his resistance and his inability to forgive took up a lot of energy. Because of the law of attraction, this negative energy was bringing in more negative energy. Unfortunately, this client didn't take any steps toward forgiveness. I found it quite sad. I have lost touch with this client, but I have prayed for his health, well-being, and ability to forgive.

When I receive the guidance that a client is stuck due to lack of forgiveness, I encourage her to begin to let go and release. Most people are unaware that being stuck is due to unfinished business. The journey to forgiveness is never an easy one, but it leads to freedom. Ask yourself this question: how much of your thoughts, energy, and time do you put into non-forgiveness: 25 percent, 35 percent, 50 percent, 85 percent? Does your inability to forgive consume your life? Does it rule your actions and behavior?

We are unable to see that our unwillingness to forgive affects our perception of the world. If you've been cheated on, you begin to view all men or women as cheaters. If your house was burglarized by a minority, you begin to view all minorities as untrustworthy. If your boss is constantly berating you, you begin to view all forms of authority as something you want to rise above. If your mother didn't nurture you and was unloving, you feel all mothers act in the same manner. If your dad was absent, you begin to view all male forms as distant. When we are stuck, our perception is jaded. When we are jaded, we are no longer able to see one isolated incident within two opposing realities anymore. We act from a place of "it's me against the world."

I have a client who repeatedly dates men who are emotionally unavailable. My client is present, open, honest, and communicative, but she feels stuck with the same type of men. During a recent session, I asked my client about her relationship with her dad. She indicated that she didn't know her dad very well. She explained that during her formative years her father had traveled a lot. She added that she typically saw him only once or twice monthly. When she saw her dad, he was always nice and kind, but he never expressed any loving feelings toward her. She told me that he often looked at her as if he were at a loss for words and that he seemed disconnected. "He was my daddy, and I wanted to know that he loved me, but he was so unavailable and distant." When my client hit her teen years, her parents divorced, and she never saw her father again. Saddened and angry, my client stuffed her feelings away and ignored the pain.

During our sessions, I explained to her the importance of making peace and forgiving her emotionally unavailable father. I told her I could see that her dad wasn't able to effectively communicate his love to her, but that he did love her. In further discussions, we focused on her desire to take on emotionally distant and unavailable men as a way to gain the love she never received from her dad. I encouraged my client to work through this issue. In time, my client was able to see how her behavior and unconscious actions enabled her to repeat the same pattern over and over. My client began to understand the importance of forgiving her father and releasing him. My client realized that this work would lead her to a place where she'd meet the right partner. Eighteen months after our work began, my client called me to say she'd met someone new. Her new partner was present and available, just as she was.

Most people don't realize that the inability to forgive ties them to the past and doesn't allow them to live in the now. They can't see that they remain stuck in old belief systems and habits. Is there someone you need to forgive? If yes, ask yourself the following questions.

1. Do you feel ready to forgive this person? If not, why?
2. What is holding you back from releasing this person from your life? Are you still angry? Hurt? Frustrated?
3. Do you think this person knows the depths to which they have hurt you?
4. Do you think this person is investing any thought or energy in your inability to forgive him or her?
5. Do you realize that you are empowering the person by being unwilling to let him or her go?
6. How long do you wish to make his or her needs more important than yours?
7. Can you understand why they behaved the way they did?
8. Do you know what this person's reality is like?
9. Can you find a way to begin the forgiveness process by at least considering how you can be free?

Is there someone who hasn't forgiven you? If yes, ask yourself these questions.

1. Do you know why this person is upset or angry with you?
2. What choice or choices did you make that led this person to feel the way they do?
3. If the shoe were on the other foot, what would you have done?
4. Are you sorry for what you did?
5. Can you forgive yourself for what you did?
6. Can you ask this person for forgiveness?

7. If presented with the situation again, what would you choose?

8. What wisdom or teachings can you take away from this experience?

9. Do you see how forgiveness will allow you to be free?

Here's another story about forgiveness. Andrew was a good-looking, dark-haired guy who came to me for a reading at a psychic fair. He wanted to know why he couldn't meet a nice, intelligent woman. He explained to me that each woman he'd dated had been self-involved and seemed uninterested in his needs. I asked Andrew about his mother and her connection to the women he was meeting. After a brief pause, he admitted that all of the women he'd dated had shared similar qualities with his mother. He said their relationship had been very challenging for him. He indicated that he'd always felt like she'd put her needs before his. Andrew's mother had raised him as a single parent. Andrew felt she'd always resented that. I asked Andrew if it would be possible to find a way to forgive his mother. He told me that the wound between them ran very deep and that he couldn't see the importance of forgiving her. I told Andrew about the law of attraction. I explained that he'd continue to attract the wrong types of women into his life until he forgave and made peace with his mother's behavior. Tears streamed down his eyes as he realized he could no longer put the blame on this mother for his challenging love life. Andrew realized he'd have to do some work in order to meet the right woman. Six months later, he followed up with me and indicated that he'd begun his forgiveness work. He said he felt lighter and was now focusing on meeting a woman who had the qualities he desired. Additionally, he admitted that he'd become more aware of the qualities he didn't want in a potential mate. I was confident that Andrew would eventually meet the right person for him.

Forgiveness, like so many other things in life, is a *choice*. We can choose today to forgive someone who hurt us five minutes ago, yesterday, or twenty-five years ago. It's the choice to accept someone else's non-perfection, accept your own non-perfection, and release the tie that binds you together that will set you free.

In forgiving someone, we see and recognize the fragility of human nature. We all know that no one is perfect. With that knowledge, we accept that we all make mistakes. If we can ask Spirit to "forgive us our trespasses," shouldn't we also ask for the strength to be able to forgive others their trespasses?

KEY POINTS FOR REFLECTION AND JOURNALING

1. Do you understand the concept of separate realities?
2. Can you see how separate realities can lead people to make choices that are often not in the best interests of others?
3. Do you see the correlation between unresolved feelings and the body's ability to manifest disease?
4. Do you understand the power of forgiveness and its ability to free you?
5. Do you feel closer to forgiving someone or asking for forgiveness? What would help you move forward with that decision?

A MEDITATION TO ASSIST THE JOURNEY

Before beginning this meditation, please have paper and a pen ready.

Find a quiet spot. Take several deep breaths. Focus on the breath going in and out of the body. Let go and release. Let go and release. Let go and release. Beginning with your toes and traveling up to the top of your head, slowly take the time to relax your body. Imagine all your stresses fading and floating away. Take several more deep breaths. When you are ready, bring your attention to your heart. Go deep into the most beautiful cavern of your heart and allow yourself to feel the love there. What color do you see here? Is it gold? Is it green? Is it pink? Is it luminescent? Allow that love to spiral out of your heart and wash over you from head to toe. Feel this love resonating and vibrating all around you. Take several deep breaths. If you need to forgive someone, bring to mind the person who hurt you. If you have hurt someone, bring to mind the person whose forgiveness you desire. Be with a vision of this person. Allow any thoughts or feelings to come to the surface. If you find yourself getting angry or emotional, take a few deep breaths and give yourself space to be with these feelings. When you are ready, begin composing a letter to this person. You will not be sending this letter to them. The purpose of this exercise is to facilitate the processing of any unresolved feelings. The letter may start in a place of anger and then progress into feelings of sorrow. The letter may start in a place of sadness, progress into feelings of liberation and then grow to anger. Allow the letter to take on a life of its own. Continue writing until the process feels finished. Please remember the following when writing the letter. Write a page and flip it over.

Do not go back and re-read it. Be true to all the emotions that come to the surface. You might find yourself brimming with anger one minute and then wallowing in tears the next. You might find yourself longing for this person or wishing that some type of harm came to them. Do not judge the feelings. They are energy. Give the experience your full attention. In order to do so, turn off your cell phone. I'd also recommend that you write with pen and paper. I do not feel this exercise is as effective when typing on a keyboard. When the letter is complete, tear it up, shred it or burn it. Again, please do not go back and re-read it. The process of re-reading it brings the energy back into you. This defeats the purpose of having released it. As you destroy the letter, state the following aloud:

'Today I choose forgiveness. I see and I know the importance of forgiveness. I have been stuck in the past. Today I step into a new future for myself. I reclaim the relationship of my dreams. I transform my energies. I shift my law of attraction qualities. I am in the proper alignment. I am grateful for the commitment I have made to myself as I walk this journey to the right relationship.'

When you are ready, return to the room and take notice of any sensations or feelings you are experiencing. If possible, take notes or record your impressions in a journal.

CHAPTER 7

MIRROR, MIRROR ON THE WALL

In the beginning of the Walt Disney classic *Snow White and the Seven Dwarfs*, we are introduced to the wicked queen. We watch as she engages in her daily consultation with her magic mirror. "Mirror, mirror on the wall, who is the fairest one of all?" she asks. Each time, the mirror replies that the wicked queen is the fairest. As a side note, the reader is told that the lovely Snow White will be safe from the queen's jealousy as long as the mirror continues to lie to her. The mirror's deceit continues until one day, when it replies, "Behold, a lovely maid I see. Rags cannot hide her gentle grace. Alas, she is more fair than thee. Lips red as the rose. Hair black as ebony. Skin white as snow." At this point, the wicked queen sees her worst fear come true. She knows that Snow White is the fairest of all. Possessed by anger and revenge, the queen sets out to have Snow White killed.

How does the story of the evil queen and Snow White relate to us? Snow White represents our ideal, or divine, self. The queen and her evil nature represent the dark, or shadow, side of our self, the aspects of our inner terrain that have gone unhealed, unnoticed, and unloved. The mirror represents and reflects those aspects of herself that the queen has been unwilling to see. In this case, the queen wants to be the fairest of all, but she cannot be the fairest while possessing such dark thoughts and energies. The mirror's admission provides the opportunity for the queen to make peace with her darkness. She refuses. In this story, the mirror is the catalyst for change. In the same respect, mirroring is a catalyst for change in our own lives. What is mirroring and its role in our lives?

Mirroring is the concept in which a person in our lives "mirrors" an unresolved or disowned aspect of ourselves that we have not been willing to face. Mirroring is a way for us to come to terms with the unresolved aspect of ourselves and make peace with it. Take a moment to think about what annoys you or upsets you about a coworker, friend, boss, or lover. The unpleasant emotion you feel in their presence is a mirror to something unresolved in yourself. Why does the mirror show us this emotion? We need to recognize the emotion within ourselves and make peace with it. In making peace with mirrored aspects of ourselves, we find that we lose attachment to them. When mirroring occurs in our intimate relationships, it is even more powerful because it is intertwined with various levels of trust between both parties. Many times a level of trust or lack thereof can trigger a reflection that leads to a major change in a relationship. The following three experiences with clients illustrate the scope of this experience.

Two days into a new year that was full of promise and hope, a client contacted me in a state of sadness. She told me that her new year had already been ruined because she'd discovered her boyfriend smoking pot at 11:50 pm on New Year's Eve. She admitted she was devastated by this revelation. I asked her to explain the circumstances of the situation.

"I knew something wasn't right when I couldn't find James anywhere at the party. It was getting closer and closer to midnight, and I didn't know where he was," she explained. I asked her what her intuition was telling her. "I had a gut feeling that I should walk out the front door, but I kept ignoring it." Finally, as the new year approached, she listened to her intuition and opened the front door. At that moment, she saw James and another woman sharing a joint. "I started screaming at him. 'What are you doing? Are you f------- nuts?' I realized everyone was watching me."

Hurt, confused, angry, and shocked, my client asked me to connect with Spirit to see what was going on. I told her I could see a lot of smoke around James and that this was not an isolated incident. Additionally, I was given a visual image of a crack in the earth. This image told me the crack related to the foundation of their relationship. As we discussed the situation further, my client indicated that the trust she'd felt for James was now broken and that she couldn't see how she'd be able to move forward with the relationship. She indicated that she'd told James that they'd need to take a time-out. She felt she needed time to figure out what to do.

During the session, we explored the dynamics of the relationship and discussed the highs and the lows. My client had been in the relationship with James for two years. During our previous work together, she'd indicated that she had provided emotional support to James, though she was financially more successful than he was. She'd expressed concern about the fact that she'd learned that his ability and desire to make money was in direct opposition to hers. Previously, we'd had several discussions about how that imbalance made her feel, and she had indicated that it made her feel quite uncomfortable. Despite the disparity in their feelings about money, she readily supported his dream to pursue his art and to open his own business. Also, she felt she had shown compassion for the fact that he'd been emotionally crippled by his upbringing.

During our discussion, I was reminded by Spirit that I had seen smoke around James in an earlier reading. In fact, I remembered seeing the smoke around him when she'd contacted me for a reading after she met James. When I'd relayed the information to my client then, she had indicated that he was not a smoker, cigarettes or other. At that time, the subject was dropped. If my client had paid attention to this visual, she may have discovered his pot-smoking problem much sooner.

Despite her early concerns about money, my client had gone forward with her relationship with James. Two years later, speechless after finding him behaving like a teenager, she only had one question for me: Why? I explained to her that she was being tested. I told her that her eyes had been opened to a part of James she hadn't seen or been willing to see. I indicated that she had a choice. She could accept James and his pot smoking, or she could terminate the relationship, begin to heal, and move forward. When she asked why she was being tested, I indicated that relationships are about accepting all aspects of someone; i.e., the things you like, the things you don't like, etc. At this time, she needed to recognize this aspect of James. Additionally, I told her this was a lesson in trust. I told her that James had been smoking pot for a long time. I asked her if she could tolerate his pot smoking. Could she learn to trust James again? Was this act the final chapter in their relationship? I told her that the ability to rebuild trust was possible if she was willing to commit to doing the work. As we ended our session, my client indicated that she had some serious soul searching to do.

To most of us, change is a terrible thing. For my client, it was the end of her world. My client would have liked to remain unaware of James's pot smoking as long as possible. Spirit had other plans. My client had been shown the chink in the armor of the knight she'd loved and supported. This wasn't tragic. It was heroic. While she felt the relationship was over, she had an opportunity to deepen the relationship and embrace this place of darkness within him or release him from her life. On a higher level, her boyfriend was saying to her, "Here is a piece of me you haven't seen yet. Can you accept it? Will you reject it? Will you reject me?" This experience provided my client an opportunity to deepen her ability to love while rebuilding a level of trust that had not been grounded in knowledge of James's full self. Her boyfriend's actions had provided my client with a mirror. Was her reaction mirroring a place within herself where she had not been truthful with him? Yes. She hadn't admitted to him her feelings about his financial instability. My client was unable to see that she had an opportunity at this point to come to terms with a disowned aspect of herself. Her boyfriend had allowed something in his dark side to present itself to her. In effect, this was a gift. "I showed you a dark piece of my inner puzzle. Will you show me one of yours?" Unconsciously he was asking her, "Can we find peace in our respective darker sides and still love each other?" Sadly, my client was so repulsed by this dark puzzle piece that her immediate reaction was to push him away. If she had been willing to go within and look closely at her own inner landscape, she may have identified the piece of her inner puzzle that needed to be brought to light.

We are often unable to see the gift that comes in the form of a problem or challenge in a relationship. We want to know why the fairy tale ended or the dream shattered. We cannot see the divinity in the events that happen to us. Sometimes the worst experience can actually bring us closer to the pot of gold at the end of the rainbow. Like the queen, we often don't like to see what is staring back at us in the mirror.

A few days later, a second client contacted me for a session. She wanted to know what was going on in the life of the man she'd dated and then told off because she felt he was distant and unavailable. As I looked at his energy, I could see that very little had changed since the previous reading. He was living his life, going to work, enjoying his hobbies, spending time with his friends, and planning a vacation. My client seemed disappointed that his life was in a status quo mode. She'd expected him to be upset, sad, depressed: in mourning because she was no longer a part of his life. As we continued our session, I asked her to explore her need for his behavior to be the way she'd wanted it to be. She told me that she'd like to see him sad and depressed about living without her. I asked if she was looking for revenge. She said she was frustrated and surprised that he had not contacted her. When I explained that she'd initiated the breakup, she replied that he could have attempted to apologize. I explained to her that that response was not in his energetic dynamic. When I added that she needed to accept him for who he was, she indicated that she'd had a hard time accepting him for who he was. She felt that there was more to him but had never seen it.

I asked her if she felt he had accepted her for who she was. She said she wasn't sure. After a pause, she indicated that she'd always put on a cheerful face in his presence but that in actuality she had been quite stressed out. She admitted that she didn't feel comfortable enough to really share with him what was going on in her life. I asked my client if she could see the mirror he provided. She shook her head. I explained that she had not been authentic with him and that he had mirrored that same in-authenticity with her. I added that her frustration and anger grew over having to maintain a mask she didn't like. I explained to my client that he'd actually been a wonderful teacher to her, but that she was not ready to accept the lesson at the time.

There are times in relationships where we fear rejection if we behave and act in accordance with how we are really feeling. When a relationship is new, we feel pressured to be in a good mood, to be happy, to feel joyous and positive, even when there are aspects in our lives that we do not feel good about. My client was unable to see that her "happy face" mask was easy to see through. Additionally, her boyfriend used his own distant mask to keep himself from truly showing who he was. While the mirror between the two of them was obvious to me, my client was unable to see how her inclination to wear a mask had led to the demise of the relationship. As long as she wore her mask and he wore his, the relationship would have revolved around falseness instead of authentic behavior.

My third client and her boyfriend had been living together for six months. He loved to work out and eat right, and he maintained a strict schedule for getting sufficient sleep every night. She was a party girl who loved to have fun, drink, and be silly. While their relationship had its share of love, joy, and mutual respect, their life-style differences caused a significant challenge to their relationship. When my client got arrested for her second DUI after an office Christmas party, her boyfriend took immediate action and moved out of their two-bedroom apartment. Upset, sad, and concerned about how to pay the rent each month, my client told me that they had been growing apart for awhile. When I asked her about his sudden departure, she said that she hadn't been drinking that much and just happened to be in the wrong place at the wrong time. As I spoke further with my client, I realized she was unable to see the seriousness of her drinking problem. In fact, she could not recognize the DUI as the catalyst through which her boyfriend ended their relationship.

On a subconscious level, my client wanted the DUI to happen to test the limits of her relationship with her boyfriend. In effect, she was saying, "Can you love me even though I have this problem?" Similarly to the incident with the other client who found her boyfriend smoking pot, my client presented an aspect of herself as a test of her boyfriend's commitment to the future of the relationship. Her boyfriend, however, unable to tolerate what had happened, took immediate action to remove himself from the situation. To him, this dark piece of her inner puzzle was something he could not bear. Unfortunately for my client, the loss of her boyfriend and the loss of her relationship were not enough for her to understand the mirror the situation provided on a conscious level. My client has now lost her license and will have to do some jail time. In addition, her job is at risk. I hope at some point that my client will be willing to do the work to identify the hidden pain that lies beneath her drinking addiction.

We can regard issues that are mirrored to us as blessings or curses. When we view the issue that the mirror shows us as a blessing, we can then search within ourselves to bring the unresolved darkness to light. When we view the image as a curse, we push away a powerful opportunity to let go of a disowned aspect of ourselves. The curses that we don't give attention to represent old emotional blocks that do not serve our current existence. These disowned aspects or pieces of our inner puzzle rise to the surface to be cleared and released. When an issue appears, we must have the desire and the commitment to release what no longer serves us. If we aren't ready, there is no judgment from Spirit. Spirit will simply provide us with another opportunity to make peace with these unresolved pieces. Our journey continues.

KEY POINTS FOR REFLECTION AND JOURNALING

1. Do you understand the concept of mirroring?
2. Can you identify the individual or individuals who are currently mirroring disowned aspects of your inner puzzle?
3. Are you aware of the knowledge contained in this puzzle piece? Can you see what you haven't been seeing?
4. Do you feel ready to release this disowned part of yourself?
5. Are you aware of the role you played in mirroring for others? Can you understand that role at this time?

A MEDITATION TO ASSIST THE JOURNEY

Find a quiet spot. Take several deep breaths. Focus on the breath going in and out of the body. Let go and release. Let go and release. Let go and release. Beginning with your toes and traveling up to the top of your head, slowly take the time to relax your body. Imagine all your stresses fading and floating away. Take several more deep breaths. When you are fully relaxed, see yourself sitting on a beautiful beach at sunset. Take another breath and allow yourself to go into a deeper place of relaxation. Just be. When you are ready, look around you. See the red ball of the sun as it begins to sink below the horizon, smell the salty air, feel the sand between your toes and hear the waves as they lap gently onto the shore. Allow yourself to feel completely at peace here. Take a moment and connect with your heart. Go deep into the most beautiful cavern of your heart and allow yourself to feel the love there. What color do you see here? Is it gold? Is it green? Is it pink? Is it luminescent? Allow that love to spiral out of your heart and wash over you from head to toe. Feel this love resonating and vibrating all around you. Take several deep breaths. Allow yourself to see a disowned piece of your inner landscape. This will be the first vision or impression you receive. What does the disowned piece feel like? Does this disowned piece have a message for you? If yes, what is the message? Do you feel ready to release this piece? If yes, state the following aloud:

'I see and acknowledge this disowned piece of my inner landscape. I allow this piece to have a voice. Today, I release this piece for once and all. I see the value that mirroring has played in my relationships. I choose to be aware of mirroring from this day forward. I reclaim the relationship of my dreams. I transform my energies. I shift my law of attraction qualities. I am in the proper alignment. I am grateful for the commitment I have made to myself as I walk this journey to the right relationship.'

When you are ready, return to the room and take notice of any sensations or feelings you are experiencing. If possible, take notes or record your impressions in a journal.

CHAPTER 8

HIT THE BULLS-EYE AND HEAL YOUR ARCHETYPES

In Caroline Myss's book *Sacred Contracts*, the reader is introduced to the four universal archetypes. What is an archetype? "A collectively inherited unconscious idea, pattern of thought, image, etc., universally present in individual psyches."[1] Once recognized and acknowledged, these universal archetypes can become allies in assisting our growth. After making peace with the universal archetypes, we can use the wisdom received from them as guideposts in our search for the right relationship. Each universal archetype has a positive and a negative, or shadow, aspect. The four universal archetypes are the child, the prostitute, the saboteur, and the victim.

---

1   Dictionary.reference.com

THE CHILD ARCHETYPE

The child archetype is subdivided into several categories: the orphan child, the magical/innocent child, the nature child, the divine child, the *puer/puella eternis*, or eternal boy/girl, and the wounded child. While some people will feel a resonance with other child categories, most people feel a strong connection to the qualities and characteristics of the wounded child, which include wounds from abuse, neglect, and trauma. Wounded children feel that the painful experiences of their childhood are closely tied to the dysfunctions they encounter in their personal and professional lives. The lesson for the wounded child is forgiveness and letting go. The shadow aspect of this archetype is self-pity and blaming one's parents for life's problems. Because the wounded child has not found a place for forgiveness, he or she will often project their issues on others. Lack of focus on healing this archetype leads the wounded child to repeatedly date and/or marry the wrong partners.

An example of the wounded child archetype can be found in Miranda's story. In my first meeting with Miranda, she boasted about the professional success she'd achieved with the assistance of her mentor. As we dove further into the session, Miranda admitted she'd been carrying on an affair with her married mentor for several years. While she knew the affair was wrong, Miranda continued to see him because she'd grown accustomed to the expensive gifts he bought her and the professional help he'd provided to her career. In return, Miranda provided this man with the emotional support he wasn't getting from his wife. Stuck, confused and reluctant to move forward, Miranda and I tapped into her wounded child. Through phone and in-person sessions, Miranda and I discussed the pain, the sadness and the unworthiness her wounded child had been carrying for years. Slowly Miranda began to see that her wounded child needed healing in order for her to have a healthy relationship with an available man.

Over a period of two years, I assisted Miranda as she worked through her wounds. At the conclusion of our sessions, Miranda had ended her relationship with her mentor on both a personal and professional level and decided to move back East to pursue a new career.

FIVE QUESTIONS FOR THE WOUNDED CHILD ARCHETYPE

1. Am I aware of my wounds? Can I see the wounded child in me?
2. Am I willing to take the necessary steps to heal my wounded child?
3. Can I see beyond the abuse, neglect, and trauma in order to create a new life for myself?
4. Do I believe that my unwillingness to let go of the past is keeping me from having the life I've dreamed of?
5. Which parent am I unwilling to forgive? What gift would I receive for forgiving this parent?

THE PROSTITUTE ARCHETYPE

The word *prostitute* brings to mind a woman prostituting herself for money. However, the prostitute archetype goes deeper. When working with this archetype, we need to look at our beliefs about integrity and self-worth. We need to ask, "Do I value myself? Do I love and respect myself?" At its core, this archetype can teach us to develop a strong level of self-esteem and self-respect. An example of the prostitute archetype can be found in Deborah's story.

Deborah married young, right out of college; she had two daughters and became a stay-at-home mom. Deborah's husband came from money, and he was also very successful in his business. With finances taken care of, Deborah got used to living easily. Deborah had many material things but lacked a spiritual sense of who she was, illustrating the expression "Money cannot buy happiness."

Over time, Deborah began to realize the emptiness of her life. While Deborah loved her children, she became frustrated with her husband's all-consuming and controlling attitude. She resented his neediness, but she rationalized his needs because he was the sole provider. After fifteen years of marriage, Deborah felt stuck. She didn't know who she was and wondered if she'd ever know herself. As her daughters grew up and became busy with friends and school, Deborah began looking for answers. Eventually, she found her way to me.

In our initial sessions, Deborah and I discussed her unhappy, unfulfilling marriage and her fear of moving beyond the place where she was stuck. Deborah admitted that she'd considered a divorce, but she could not rationalize the loss of financial security, status, and physical safety. Deborah was uneasy and anxiety-ridden when she considered giving up the benefits of the marriage to satisfy questions like, "Who am I? Is there more for me? Is there another life for me? Is there another partner for me?"

When I explained the prostitute archetype to Deborah, she had a hard time believing that she'd sold herself out. I explained to Deborah that she needed to understand the prostitute archetype, acknowledge its teachings, and make peace with it. I added that working through this archetype and its corresponding feelings of low self-esteem and self-respect would allow her to birth a new, more confident self.

Over a number of sessions, Deborah began to find herself. Through meditation, soul searching, and yoga, she began to walk a spiritual path. She also began to see that she had her own needs and desires. Deborah took a part-time job and began maintaining her own checkbook and finances. Slowly, over time, Deborah made peace with the prostitute archetype. Nine months into our work together, Deborah asked her husband if he'd attend marriage counseling sessions. When he refused, she asked for a trial separation. At the time, both of her daughters were in college. They took the news badly. With her husband living elsewhere, Deborah found herself on her own for the first time in her life. Frightened, unsure, and confused about what was next, Deborah took baby steps and lived life one day at a time.

During that time, the prostitute archetype made several attempts to rear its ugly head. Deborah found herself having moments in which she'd wish for the financial security and the discomfort of her old life. However, she knew there was no turning back. After one year of separation, Deborah told her husband she wanted a divorce. Deborah felt the prostitute archetype return when she struggled and agonized over finding herself a lawyer to file the requisite papers.

Over time, Deborah found the strength to hire a lawyer. As Deborah's attorney and her husband's attorney began discussions regarding dissolving the marriage and splitting the assets, Deborah called me and said she was thinking of taking her husband back and moving forward as if this self-determined period had been a bad dream. I explained to Deborah that this was her final test. The prostitute archetype was attempting a last-ditch effort. During our session, I asked her to take a look at all the work she'd done to make herself independent and autonomous. I also talked to her about the spiritual path she was walking and praised her choice to build a new life for herself.

A few days later, Deborah contacted me to say that she'd worked through her fears and was moving forward with the divorce. Today, Deborah is divorced from her husband. She is dating a new man, working in a different career, and selling her home. She's grateful for her journey.

FIVE QUESTIONS FOR THE PROSTITUTE ARCHETYPE

1. Can I see the prostitute archetype in my life?
2. Am I willing to take the necessary steps to heal the prostitute archetype? If not, why not?
3. How willing am I to prostitute myself in order to maintain the financial security or status I've attained in a relationship?
4. How willing am I to sell my power to someone else?
5. How willing am I to buy an interest in someone else in order to gain power or status?

THE SABOTEUR ARCHETYPE

Similar in dynamic to the prostitute version, the saboteur archetype involves low self-esteem. In the negative, or shadow, aspect of this archetype, we make decisions that sabotage ourselves or others. While you can self-sabotage or sabotage others in every area of your life, we frequently sabotage ourselves in our romantic relationships. This is the place where we "settle" by:

a. Dating a man or woman who isn't what we are looking for
b. Dating someone who keeps us company because we don't want to be alone

In our choice to settle, we sabotage ourselves by not aspiring to the relationship we truly desire. Additionally, when we put ourselves into unhealthy dating situations, we can be sabotaged by others. For example, if you are involved with someone who only wants your emotional, physical, or financial support, you are allowing yourself to be sabotaged. In cases when the partnership is unequal and unbalanced, one party gives all their love and support to another party and receives little or nothing in return, or one party financially supports another party and in return demands that the relationship be in accordance with their terms.

An example of the saboteur archetype can be found in Pauline's story. Pauline had turned forty the day before she came for a reading with me. Surprised to be forty years old and a single mom of two young girls, Pauline was looking for information about a man she'd been seeing who was significantly younger than her. When I focused on this man's energy, I knew he'd be trouble.

"He lacks focus, doesn't have a solid career and likes to party." I explained.

"Yes, he works landscaping during the day and drinks almost every night." she said.

"He's doing a lot more than drinking. I see pills. I see smoke. He does drugs." I said.

"Yes, he likes to party and I've been partying with him." she said.

"What do you hope to get out of this situation?" I asked.

"I'm not sure. He's fun, he likes my girls, the sex is amazing; but I'm reluctant to ask for anything more because he's not really in the right space or place." she said.

"You've been doing a lot of drugs, haven't you?" I asked.

"Yes." she said.

"Did you pass out?" I asked.

"Yes, I was drinking and I took some pills. I passed out at this party we were at." she said.

"You're taking a lot of risks. Can you see that?" I said.

"What do you mean?" she asked.

"You're dating a young guy who has an addiction problem, you've brought him into your home to meet your girls, you are having sex with him and you're doing a lot of drugs. Aren't you worried about how this behavior will affect your life and your girls?" I asked.

"I'm really into this guy. I'm telling you – the sex is the best I've ever had in my life. It's like we're connected somehow." she said.

"Yes, that is the past life I see between the two of you, however he hasn't changed much since the last time you were with him." I said.

"I don't know what to do. I'd like something more, but I don't think he's ready." she said.

As she spoke to me, I began to see the red flashing lights of a cop car and then I saw an image of Pauline behind bars. I had a very uncomfortable feeling about these visions.

"Pauline, you need to be careful. I'm feeling like there is a strong possibility you could be arrested and end up in jail." I said.

"What? Why?" she asked.

"I think its one of those situations where you are in the wrong place at the wrong time. This has to do with this guy you are dating." I said.

"I can't go to jail. What about my girls? What would happen to them? My ex would have a fit, if I ended up in jail." she said.

"I really think you need to be careful of where you go and what you do with this guy." I said.

"Oh my God! I can't believe this." she said.

"Please be careful." I added.

I heard from Pauline one or two more times after that session and then she didn't contact me again. I do not know what happened to her. I found it unfortunate that Pauline could not see the saboteur archetype at work in her life. If she had been willing to look at the way in which the saboteur was running her life, she may have been able to turn things around. I've prayed for her safety.

FIVE QUESTIONS FOR THE SABOTEUR ARCHETYPE

1. Have I been sabotaged in a relationship? If yes, how do I feel about it?

2. Can I forgive myself? Can I forgive the person(s)?
3. Have I self-sabotaged in a relationship. If yes, how do I feel about it?
4. Can I forgive myself? Can I forgive the other people who played roles in the drama?
5. If I can see the saboteur in me, am I willing to make that aspect an ally and learn from its' teachings?

THE VICTIM ARCHETYPE

The victim's dark side is evident; however, the victim has a powerful lesson for us. Once healed, the victim befriends us by letting us know when we are on the verge of being victimized and when we are about to victimize someone else. The shadow aspect of the victim can be found in those individuals who use victimization to foster sympathy, pity, and empathy from others. Such people find power by hiding behind the archetype and using its energies in a negative way.

Catelynn's story provides an example of the victim archetype and the power it wields on our lives. Catelynn and Matt worked for a large company together. While they were acquainted with one another and said hello from time to time, they worked in different departments. During a reading, Catelynn, asked about Matt. I told her that I could see that he had a girlfriend or love interest because there was a feminine energy around him. Catelynn said that she'd heard about his girlfriend from another employee. When she inquired about the possibility of something happening between her and Matt, I explained that he was involved and that she should leave the situation alone.

Several months later, Catelynn was offered a new job opportunity in another company. While Catelynn felt sad to leave her position, she could not pass up the job and its amazing potential. Through the grapevine, Matt heard that Catelynn had given notice and would be leaving the company soon. At that point, Matt approached Catelynn and asked her if she'd like to go out on a date. Surprised by his request, Catelynn inquired about his girlfriend. Matt explained that they'd been on and off for quite some time and that he had asked the woman to stop contacting him. As Catelynn listened to Matt's story, she felt queasy. Her stomach became upset, and she felt nauseous. Catelynn later told me that she felt like her gut was warning her to stay away from Matt, but she didn't listen to the message she was receiving.

A few days later, Catelynn and Matt went out on a date. Catelynn had a wonderful time. She bragged to her friends that she was looking forward to seeing Matt again. As her time at her current job wound down, Catelynn found herself feeling sad that she would be moving forward. She realized she would miss seeing Matt around the office. Despite her uncertainties about her situation with Matt, Catelynn began spending a lot of time with him.

In conversations about old relationships, Catelynn learned that Matt's ex-girlfriend, Wendy, had been 100 percent financially dependent on Matt. Additionally, Wendy had few friends and spent all her time with Matt. Catelynn felt she could provide Matt with a different type of relationship. She believed they could be equals who loved and supported each other. In many ways, Catelynn, who had a career, friends, interests, and a loving family environment, felt superior to Wendy.

In our session, Catelynn explained how excited she was to participate in a relationship in which both partners were equals. I explained to Catelynn that some men prefer a superior role in a relationship and that Matt might not want to be an equal. I added that the illusion of control in a relationship can be very appealing to some men. This approach makes love between both parties conditional. Catelynn was so excited to be involved with Matt that she wasn't paying attention to her gut. When I asked her why she was ignoring her gut, she admitted feeling queasy. She also expressed her uncertainty. I told Catelynn that I was sensing Wendy's energies around Matt. Catelynn told me she was not aware of any contact between Matt and Wendy.

A few weeks later, during an intimate moment between Matt and Catelynn in his apartment, Wendy showed up and began banging on the front door. Startled, surprised, and shocked, Catelynn immediately observed a shift in Matt's demeanor. After going to the door and talking with Wendy, Matt returned and asked Catelynn to leave. Unsure of what to do, Catelynn decided to stay. As if a faucet was turned off, Matt ignored Catelynn. Catelynn spent the night on the couch and then went home. When Catelynn did not hear from Matt for several days, she contacted me for a session.

During our meeting, Catelynn explained the recent occurrences. I could feel how spiritually, psychically, and emotionally fragile she was. The first message I received was that it wasn't over yet and that Catelynn would hear from Matt in the next few days. Catelynn was surprised by this information. I told her he'd reach out to her, and I asked what she'd do when he contacted her. Catelynn admitted she didn't know what to do. She told me how lost she felt. She couldn't understand why Matt had lied to her about his ex, why he had shut down the way he did, or why he asked her to leave. Tears streamed down her face. I asked Catelynn why she'd ignored her gut. She had no answer for me. I explained that her lesson in this situation was to listen to her gut, her intuition. I explained that her intuition had tried to warn her about Matt from the beginning and that she should not have gotten involved with him.

"Do you feel like you got this lesson?" I asked.

"I don't know," Catelynn answered.

"It is important that you understand this lesson and what it has to teach you. If you don't get it, you'll have to repeat the lesson until it is complete. Make sense?" I said.

"Why would he continue to be so receptive and open to a needy woman?" Catelynn asked.

I explained to Catelynn that it was obvious that Matt did not want a relationship in which he was an equal party. He appeared to enjoy having the upper hand because it gave him a sense of control.

"Well, if that's what he wants, why did he date me?" Catelynn asked.

I explained that there was a part of Matt that wanted to be with her and was willing to give the relationship a shot, even though it would mean that the two of them were on equal footing.

"He tried, but at the end of the day he couldn't do it. He was more comfortable in his superior role. I know you are hurt, but there is a beautiful lesson here. In time, you'll need to forgive Matt and forgive yourself," I explained.

"I can't bear to think about that right now," Catelynn said.

Matt showed up, unannounced, at Catelynn's house a few days later. They reconciled briefly, and then Matt dumped her again. That time, Catelynn swore she wouldn't go back. It was over.

Catelynn couldn't see that her decision to date Matt was the result of not paying attention to her gut, or intuition. When the situation turned negative, Catelynn went into victim mode. She repeatedly blamed Matt instead of looking at her own choices. Catelynn connected with the shadow aspect of the victim by asking why this had happened to her. She couldn't see her own role in the situation. Matt, on the other hand, proved to be a powerful teacher for her. His presence in her life provided an opportunity for her to be more in tune with her own internal wisdom and make peace with her victim archetype. Catelynn's teachings in this area are ongoing.

FIVE QUESTIONS FOR THE VICTIM ARCHETYPE

1. Can I see situations in which I have been a victim?
2. Did I embrace the shadow aspect of the victim? How do I feel about that situation now?

3. Am I in tune with my internal wisdom, or intuition? If yes, how has it helped me? If no, why do I ignore it?
4. Take a moment and look at a troubling situation in your current life. Can you become a victim in this situation?
5. Do you believe that you have the ability to victimize someone? If no, why not?

As you can see, the wounded child, the prostitute, the saboteur, and the victim archetypes are powerful unconscious influences that have the ability to affect our law of attraction and ultimately the people we date, love, and want to marry.

KEY POINTS FOR REFLECTION AND JOURNALING

1. Can I see the role that each archetype plays in my life?
2. Is there one, or more, archetypes that I am resisting looking at and working on? If yes, why?
3. Pick one of the archetypes you are feeling resistance to and journal your feelings. Do you feel sad, angry, disgusted, or frustrated?
4. If you've begun to make peace with one of the archetypes, how does it affect the way you perceive yourself and the way you perceive your relationships?
5. If you experienced a potential love interest engaging with the negative aspect of one of the archetypes, what would you do? How do you think it would feel to witness this process?

A MEDITATION TO ASSIST THE JOURNEY

Find a quiet spot. Take several deep breaths. Focus on the breath going in and out of the body. Let go and release. Let go and release. Let go and release. Beginning with your toes and traveling up to the top of your head, slowly take the time to relax your body. Imagine all your stresses fading and floating away. Take several more deep breaths. When you are fully relaxed, see yourself sitting on a beautiful beach at sunset. Take another breath and allow yourself to go into a deeper place of relaxation. Just be. When you are ready, look around you. See the red ball of the sun as it begins to sink below the horizon, smell the salty air, feel the sand between your toes and hear the waves as they lap gently onto the shore. Allow yourself to feel completely at peace here. Take a moment and connect with your heart. Go deep into the most beautiful cavern of your heart and allow yourself to feel the love there. What color do you see here? Is it gold? Is it green? Is it pink? Is it luminescent? Allow that love to spiral out of your heart and wash over you from head to toe. Feel this love resonating and vibrating all around you. Take several deep breaths. Allow yourself to connect with the energies of the archetype you dislike. Is it the wounded child? It is the prostitute? Is it the saboteur? Is it the victim? Go deep into your feelings and connect with this archetype. Do you see examples of this unresolved archetype? Will you allow space for this archetype to assist you in your journey to the right relationship? When you are ready, state the following aloud:

'I acknowledge the presence of the four universal archetypes in my life. I choose to work through the shadow aspects of these archetypes. I choose to embrace the teachings of these archetypes. I see the role these archetypes have played in my relationships. If I cannot see the role of a specific archetype and its influence in my life, I ask that it be revealed to me via meditation, journaling or in the dreamtime. I reclaim the relationship of my dreams. I transform my energies. I shift my law of attraction qualities. I put myself in the proper alignment. I am grateful for the commitment I have made to myself as I walk this journey to the right relationship.'

When you are ready, return to the room and take notice of any sensations or feelings you are experiencing. If possible, take notes or record your impressions in a journal.

CHAPTER 9

PLEASE CLAIM YOUR BAGGAGE AT CAROUSEL NUMBER ONE

Baggage. For most people the word *baggage* has two definitions: the luggage we bring on a trip and the unfinished emotional business that everyone carries around from childhood. We all have baggage. Not one person on the planet doesn't own some type of baggage, and yet a large percentage of the population ignores their baggage. Why? They don't want to deal with it. They don't want to dredge it up and look it in the eye, make peace with it, and move on. For many people, baggage is something they'd like to stick in the back of their closet and forget about. Most people don't realize that their unfinished baggage affects their day-to-day behavior and thoughts.

Ask yourself the following questions about baggage:

- What thoughts and perceptions about myself do I "carry" around?
- What old tapes or movies do I continue to play in my head?
- What do I dislike about myself?
- What events keep me with one foot in the past?
- What regrets do I have?
- Who am I unwilling to forgive or release? Why?
- What old hurts, disappointments, or resentments am I tightly clinging to?
- What am I disgraced about?
- What makes me sick about looking in the mirror?
- What beliefs do I have about myself that are limiting?

Because we are reluctant to deal with our own baggage, the bar is raised when dealing with baggage brought into relationships. For many people, the choice to stay in a relationship or let it go revolves around whether or not they want to deal with their partner's baggage. They ask themselves, "Is this worth it or should I walk away?"

Ask yourself if these are baggage issues that you'd dislike in a partner:

- Is he divorced? How do I feel about that?
- Does he have kids? How do I feel about that?
- Is she coming from another relationship into a relationship with me? How do I feel about that?
- Is she good at taking care of herself? If not, how do I feel about that?
- Is he too close with his family? How do I feel about that?
- Is he not close enough with his family? How do I feel about that?
- Has she made peace with the parent she felt didn't love or appreciate her? If not, why?

- Does she seem needy or distant? How do I feel about that?
- Overall, is he in touch with his baggage? Does he talk about it? How do I feel about his baggage? Can I live with it? Would I be better off without it?

Baggage comes in many forms: emotional, physical, psychological, and spiritual. Where do you carry most of your baggage? Where does your partner or potential partner carry most of his or her baggage?

Emotional baggage. Emotional baggage is about our feelings. Do you carry negative feelings and images of yourself, others, or both? Do you have distortions in your thoughts or feelings based on anger, sadness, grief, or guilt? Do you view men or women stereotypically, based on previous relationship disappointments? For example, are all men losers or all women needy? Do you have feelings of being stuck or feel hopeless or disillusioned about life, yourself, your purpose, and your goals?

Feelings that are buried deep within manifest in the way you present yourself to the world. Are you suspicious of others? Do you think someone is out to get you? Do you shut yourself off? Are you distant? Do you feel pent-up anger or tears that you are afraid to release? Are you afraid of being emotionally overwhelmed? Are you ready to explode at any time? What would happen if you did explode? Do you live your live safely, knowing that you are in control? Do you choose who to talk to, who to ignore, and who to gossip about? Does that behavior give you a sense of belonging, or does it alienate you?

Take a moment to think about who you are within a relationship. What emotional role have you played? Do you give everything and then feel angry for not getting as much back? Do you expect too much and get little in return? Is it all about you instead of the relationship? Has the role you've played been successful? Have you felt like a failure? Who are you when you aren't in a relationship?

How do you feel about yourself? Are you happy to be single? Do you need to be in a relationship to feel better about yourself?

Physical baggage. Physical baggage is tied to emotional baggage and is revealed in the way you feel about and treat your physical body. How do you feel about your physical body? Is it a work of art that you appreciate? Is it a machine that you expect to function efficiently and effectively? Is it a nasty, ugly thing that just happens to house your soul while you live on the planet? Do you feel connected to your body? Do you know how amazing it is that your body functions in the way that it does? Do you appreciate the body that you have? Do you take care of your body by working out, eating right, and getting adequate rest? Do you neglect your body by not exercising, eating bad food, and getting inadequate rest?

For most people, the treatment of the body falls into two categories: a temple that is respected and treated graciously or a garbage dump that takes on all the things we don't want to deal with. For many people, physical baggage occurs when they eat too much food, drink too much alcohol, smoke too many cigarettes, or take too many drugs. After years of abuse, physical baggage takes its toll on the body in the forms of obesity, diabetes, alcoholism, drug addiction, liver problems, emphysema, etc. We are all born with beautiful bodies. Why would we abuse them? We abuse our bodies because we don't want to feel. Our bodies have the capacity to feel the highest of highs, like love, happiness, joy, and euphoria. And our bodies have the capacity to feel the lowest of lows, like depression, sadness, loneliness, and alienation. At some point in our lives, we may make the choice to never feel pain. We know that painful thoughts can debilitate us. However, when we make the decision to block negative emotions, we also block the positive emotions.

Emotions are energies that need to be cleared. Because we are unwilling to face difficult emotions, we look for an outside substance that will help us dull them. When we realize its effectiveness, we believe that this source will work as long as we continue to introduce it into the body. However, the substance becomes a source of addiction that must be fed over and over again. Within every person who smokes too much, drinks too much, takes drugs, or eats to excess is an emotion he or she doesn't want to feel. Such abuse helps overcome the emotion — until the body shuts down. When disease develops, it is usually the result of physical baggage that has gone unacknowledged for too long.

Psychological baggage. Psychological baggage is tied to emotional baggage. How do we perceive ourselves? How do we perceive others? How do we perceive the world around us? Our perceptions are shaped by our life experiences. While many of us have pleasant memories, we also have memories that are less than pleasant. If you were molested, raped, beaten, abused, victimized, criticized, mocked, judged, made to feel inadequate or stupid or insufficient during childhood, you carry psychological baggage. One small incident, one large incident, or several incidences spread throughout your life can shape you and how you see others. Are you aware of this baggage? If yes, did you take the time to heal from those experiences? Did you seek out counseling? If you didn't take the time to heal from such experiences, you are still carrying them with you. You may no longer give thought to them, but they remain a part of your energetic makeup.

As long as these feelings and perceptions are unacknowledged, your ability to perceive the world is altered. Yes, the threat may be gone, but a part of you can still perceive the potential fear, anger, pain, or hurt. Left untreated, this baggage remains your lens to the world. This type of baggage impedes your ability to move forward on your path and inhibits you from evolving spiritually.

Spiritual baggage. Spiritual baggage is linked to emotional, physical, and psychological baggage. When we are feeling bad or negative, we don't take care of our physical selves. When we

aren't taking care of our physical selves, we have a tainted perception of the world. When our viewpoint of the world is altered,
we question our belief in Spirit. This process is often two-fold. At
first, you begin to wonder about the existence of Spirit. *Is Spirit
there? Is Spirit real or make-believe? Can Spirit see me? Is Spirit aware
of me?* Second, we cannot understand why Spirit isn't helping
us with our pain. We ask, "Am I important to Spirit? Do I matter to Spirit? Why isn't Spirit helping me? I know I need Spirit's
help, but nothing is happening." At this point, I've seen several
clients turn their backs on Spirit altogether. This decision to turn
their backs on Spirit comes from a place where their perception
of Spirit is jaded. Spirit is always helping us and always assisting
us. It is usually when things are at their worst that we feel we
need Spirit the most, and yet Spirit is already lovingly guiding us
through our pain. Sadly, we can't perceive the guidance or the love.
Most people maintain a love/hate relationship with their baggage.
They want to be rid of it but often find comfort in it. Our baggage
is our own, and it is familiar. We may not like our baggage, but it
provides a safety net. The longer we hold onto our baggage, the
safer we are, the more protected we feel. While our soul will urge
us to walk our path, let go of our baggage, and embrace the divine
plan for us, most people don't want to embrace the work involved
in letting go of the baggage. The ego will taunt us by saying, "Isn't
it easier to just hang onto the baggage and skip the work? Life is so
much simpler that way."

The 2010 film *The Backup Plan* offers a perfect example of what
happens when we ignore our baggage and attempt to move forward
to the next phase of our life without doing the work. The film stars
Jennifer Lopez as Zoe, a young woman who has been unable to
meet the right man. After a series of broken relationships Zoe decides to raise a child on her own and opts for artificial insemination.
After Zoe's procedure is completed, she walks out of the office to

hail a cab in rainy New York City, and she meets Stan. Played by Alex O'Loughlin, Stan appears to be the "one" for Zoe. Zoe and Stan begin to date and get to know each other. During this time, Zoe finds out that the artificial insemination procedure was successful. She is pregnant. Happy to be pregnant but feeling bittersweet, Zoe realizes she needs to explain her situation to Stan. In an effort to avoid doing so, Zoe begins to act strangely. At this point, the audience begins to see that Zoe is not in touch with her abandonment issues. Zoe has a very difficult time letting people get close to her. The audience is shown that Zoe has only a few friends and that she runs a small business with only two employees. Everyone around her can see that Zoe has been very successful in keeping people at arm's length so no one can hurt her.

Zoe's unresolved baggage and her perception of the world have convinced her that Stan will disappear from her life when he learns about her pregnancy. When Zoe finally admits her pregnancy to Stan, she is surprised when he commits to her. As the story moves forward, both Zoe and Stan realize they do not know each other outside of Zoe's pregnant state. As Zoe gets bigger and more emotional, she is unable to see how her behavior is affecting her relationship with Stan. Stan has made it clear that he is committed and ready to be with her, but Zoe wavers, waiting for him to jump ship.

After a huge argument and a parting of ways, Zoe realizes she must change in order to have Stan. Zoe's realization that she needs to let Stan in and let go of her baggage is a critical moment in this character's journey. She decides to approach Stan about a reconciliation at the same time she begins to go into labor. Shortly thereafter, Zoe has the baby and reunites with Stan. As the movie winds up, Zoe and Stan get engaged. There is a hint that Zoe is pregnant again, with Stan's baby.

While Zoe's journey ended with the relationship and the baby, her baggage of not letting anyone get close to her is not over. In her efforts to be with Stan, Zoe worked through her abandonment baggage on one level. Her work will continue in this area until the wound is healed. During her processing, Zoe attempted to project her baggage onto Stan. In her projection, she kept saying that Stan would abandon her. Zoe tried to make Stan the victimizer and remain the victim of the cycle she'd been unable to see all along. Zoe scoffed at Stan's baggage, but in fact, it wasn't his baggage at all. The baggage was hers. Why is it that we take issue with someone else's baggage? We think, *Oh my! I don't want to deal with that. That's a nightmare!* Making the decision to face our baggage and heal from it enables us to be more willing to accept the baggage of others.

How do you lighten your load? First, you must be willing and ready to do so. You must want to be rid of what no longer serves you and be ready to embrace your new life. Secondly, you need to be willing to look at yourself, your actions, and your behaviors to understand how the role you have played in carrying your baggage. It's very easy to point to the people in your life who have been unlovable, unavailable, disconnected, or detached; but you need to accept responsibility for your role in the drama. Thirdly, you need to forgive and release. Forgive those who have hurt you, harmed you, disappointed you, who didn't love you or treated you badly. Didn't they have baggage too? It is only through forgiving and releasing that you truly set yourself free.

Finally, you need to include Spirit in this decision. Pray for healing, pray for release, pray for the strength and courage to move forward. Light candles, commune with the Divine, and ask that Spirit help you in this process. Once you have done all these things, you'll feel comfortable enough to leave the baggage at the airport carousel and walk away. You know there are no tags on the baggage so it won't find its way back to you.

Letting go of the baggage creates an opening in our lives — a beautiful opening through which we can fully embrace our paths, fill the space with love, joy, and beauty, and open ourselves to meeting someone special.

KEY POINTS FOR REFLECTION AND JOURNALING

1. Do you understand baggage and the role it plays in your life?
2. Can you find an example in which your baggage has kept you safe?
3. Do you comprehend the different types of baggage? Where does your baggage fit in?
4. How do you feel about the baggage of a potential partner?
5. Are you ready to release your baggage and move forward?

A MEDITATION TO ASSIST THE JOURNEY

Find a quiet spot. Take several deep breaths. Focus on the breath going in and out of the body. Let go and release. Let go and release. Let go and release. Beginning with your toes and traveling up to the top of your head, slowly take the time to relax your body. Imagine all your stresses fading and floating away. Take several more deep breaths. When you are fully relaxed, see yourself sitting on a beautiful beach at sunset. Take another breath and allow yourself to go into a deeper place of relaxation. Just be. When you are ready, look around you. See the red ball of the sun as it begins to sink below the horizon, smell the salty air, feel the sand between your toes and hear the waves as they lap gently onto the shore. Allow yourself to feel completely at peace here. Take a moment and connect with your heart. Go deep into the most beautiful cavern of your heart and allow yourself to feel the love there. What color do you see here? Is it gold? Is it green? Is it pink? Is it luminescent? Allow that love to spiral out of your heart and wash over you from head to toe. Feel this love resonating and vibrating all around you. Take several deep breaths. Allow yourself to connect with your baggage. Is your baggage emotional? Is it physical? Is it psychological? Is it spiritual? Is it a combination? How does your baggage make you feel? Would you like to begin the work to release your baggage? If yes, take a few moments and make a silent commitment to yourself. If no, come back to this meditation when you feel more open to working through this issue. When you are ready, state the following aloud:

'I am aware of my baggage. I am aware of the way in which my baggage has affected who I am, what I am and the way I conduct myself in relationships. I live my life my way. Baggage no longer defines me. I release my baggage for once and all. I reclaim the relationship of my dreams. I transform my energies. I shift my law of attraction qualities. I put myself in the proper alignment. I am grateful for the commitment I have made to myself as I walk this journey to the right relationship.'

When you are ready, return to the room and take notice of any sensations or feelings you are experiencing. If possible, take notes or record your impressions in a journal.

CHAPTER 10

THE NO-NOS

Over the years of doing readings, I have found that most people begin a relationship with certain no-nos. What is a no-no? A no-no is a thought, an expectation, or a feeling that is brought to a relationship based on past experiences. Walking into a new relationship with one or several no-nos leads to disappointment. Three common no-nos are listed below.

- No-No 1: Having expectations
- No-No 2: Bringing needs and neediness
- No-No 3: Wearing a mask

NO-NO 1: HAVING EXPECTATIONS

In the early stage of a relationship, neither party is certain of his or her role. During this period, both parties attempt to find common ground. In time, unspoken rules develop. However, it is not uncommon for each party to step into the relationship expecting the other party to do something for them. In return, they will do something back. In this respect, the situation is similar to bartering. For example, "You take care of me, and I'll have sex with you." "You love me, and I'll raise your children." The relationship continues at this level for a period of four to six months. At some point, when the rules have been defined, the woman may realize that the other party is not meeting her expectations, and she becomes angry and resentful. Underneath the anger is pain, the feeling that her needs are not important enough to her partner. Realistically, she was incorrect in placing an expectation on that person to begin with.

This proves to be a critical point in many relationships. Now that the bubble has been shattered, can the relationship move forward? In many situations, the party who is upset is unable to see how she's created her own unhappiness by having an expectation. No one person could or should meet our expectations.

Expectations are unconscious. Expectations are a part of who and what we are, an aspect of the person we see in the mirror each morning, and they are part of the way we perceive the world. As previously discussed, we all have separate realities. Our reality is filled with expectations of what a potential partner should give to us. We cannot change these expectations until we choose to change our level of reality by changing our thoughts, and that decision to change our thoughts must come with a level of commitment to paying attention to what we are thinking, acknowledging our thoughts, understanding their message, comprehending the meaning behind the message, and actively shifting how we think. When we reach the point that our thoughts are in alignment with our real selves, they will not include expectations that we believe others should fulfill.

Here's an example of unmet expectations. There's an episode of the hilarious comedy *Sex and the City* called "Great Sexpectations."

The show centers around four New York City professional women who search for love in modern Manhattan. In this episode, Carrie (played by Sarah Jessica Parker) is dating Jack Berger, a writer. Carrie, also a writer, perceives this about the relationship: "We are two writers who have so much to talk about; we are both so knowledgeable about writing; we have such great kisses; the time we spend together is great; but the sex is quiet." The sex is so quiet that Carrie can hear the doors of the M11 bus close and open. If you have visited New York City, you know that it's difficult to hear bus doors closing at any hour of the day because of all the surrounding noise. In this situation, Carrie expected the sex would be fabulous because everything else in the relationship was fabulous. Carrie had an expectation, and she ended up very disappointed. Jack Berger's reality is never shown to the viewer, but it is obviously different from Carrie's. In his reality the sex might have been fabulous, or maybe it was so quiet that it proved to be deafening for him. Despite her unhappiness, Carrie forges ahead with the relationship. Jack, on the other hand, doesn't. The viewer is told in a later episode that Jack breaks up with Carrie via a sticky note, which Carrie finds deplorable.

The best way to go into a relationship is without expectations. Expect nothing and receive everything. How is that possible? Go into a situation in a spirit of openness. Expect nothing from the situation and nothing from the person. Be in the moment — you will be surprised. Why? Because you are in a place of not wanting or needing anything in return. Overall, this approach will provide a better experience for you. You may actually feel happier about yourself as a result of the fact that you don't need or want anything from that person or situation. When you stop expecting, you stop giving birth to unhappy outcomes in your life. When you stop birthing negativity, you allow yourself to birth a joyous relationship.

NO-NO 2: BRINGING NEEDS AND NEEDINESS

Men and women are equally guilty of requiring certain needs to be met or fulfilled when entering into a relationship. A large percentage of women enter into a relationship with the requirement that they be taken care of. Many women have told me over the years that they want a man for financial support. My question to them: "Are you looking for a spouse or a sugar daddy?" Often, men will say that they want a woman who can cook, clean, and take care of them. My question to them: "Are you looking for a wife or a maid?"

When we step into a relationship under the illusion that he's going to fill this need or she's going to fill that need, we delude ourselves into thinking that the other person's ability to fill our needs will make us happy. We are relying on them to bring us joy. We cannot see that we are looking outside ourselves for happiness. The key to a wonderful relationship is to be in touch with your own inner joy before entering a relationship.

The law of attraction says like attracts like. I cannot overstress the importance of the law of attraction and its role in dating. When we apply the law of attraction to our lives, we ultimately make peace with ourselves. Once we make peace with ourselves, we'll be in the right position to draw in someone who is also at peace with themselves. The path to a wonderful relationship begins when we are whole human beings; then the arrival of another person into our lives is icing on the cake.

Hollywood is often responsible for perpetuating misconceptions about relationship needs. In the opening scene of the 2009 film, *He's Just Not That Into You*, Gigi, played by Ginnifer Goodwin, is out on a date with Conor, played by Kevin Connolly. At the end of the date, Conor tells Gigi, "It was nice meeting you." Hearing this affirmation from the man she likes, Gigi becomes excited. She anticipates receiving a phone call. Conor, on the other hand, says good-bye to Gigi and decides not to make contact with her. Several days go by; we watch Gigi obsessively check her phone every two seconds in anticipation of Conor's phone call. When he doesn't call, Gigi leaves him a silly message. Conor does not respond. Shortly after that, Gigi arrives at Conor's local watering hole, hoping to run into him. She claims she is there to return his pen. Gigi meets the manager of the bar, Alex, played by Justin Long, and explains her dilemma to him. Alex explains to Gigi that Conor didn't call because "he's not into you." Somewhat confused but excited, Gigi leaves the bar, feeling like she just figured out what dating is all about.

Several days later, we see Gigi and her girlfriend at happy hour. Gigi is talking to an attractive lawyer who decides to make his exit to return to the office. He asks Gigi for her card and in turn gives her his card. As he's walking away he says to Gigi, "Looking forward to hearing from you." Gigi doesn't understand the dating etiquette again and runs after him to ask if that means he'll call her or if she is to call him. He responds with "We'll talk. We'll get in touch," and he leaves. Gigi initially tears up his card and proclaims to her girlfriend that she isn't going to call him. Later we see Gigi taping the card back together. She considers whether or not to call him. In desperation, Gigi contacts Alex, who advises her not to call the man because he isn't into her. Gigi backs off.

To the audience, Gigi's neediness is apparent. Gigi is so desperate for a loving relationship that she is unable to see that neither guy had any interest in her at all. Gigi is in love with the notion of being "in love." The movie details Gigi's other failed attempts at dating. All her efforts lead to the same conclusion: a needy woman. In her reality, Gigi feels that she should continue to put herself out in the dating scene with the hope that the right person will come along. Sadly, Gigi is unable to see that she needs to fully love and appreciate herself before anyone else can do so.

Conor, on the other hand, can't understand why Anna, played by Scarlet Johansson, isn't interested in sleeping with him anymore.

He spends more than half the movie in a state of confusion about this. When he finally confronts Anna about their lack of a physical relationship, she concedes to his advance. In the next scene, we see Anna lying uncomfortably in his arms. The next day, Conor brings Anna to a townhouse he's looking to buy. As they stand in the kitchen, he offers her a new life. Anna comes clean and admits that while this represents the life any woman would want, she doesn't want it with him. At that point, Anna leaves Conor alone. Conor's character is almost as translucent as Gigi. His neediness is based on the fact that he felt he had to have a committed relationship before he could take things in his life to the next level. In both situations, Conor and Gigi felt that outside influences would make them happy instead of first seeking their own inner happiness.

NO-NO 3: WEARING A MASK

Every time we step into a new relationship, we don a mask. In many cases, we put on a mask that closely mirrors what we think the other person wants us to be.

- "She wants me to be the strong, supportive type. That's what I'll show her."
- "He needs me to be pleasing, agreeable, and easy-going. That's what I'll show him."

Wearing a mask is effective for only a short period of time. Why? Our soul and spirit do not like to be shadowed. In time, one of the partners in a relationship takes off the mask, and the problems begin. He has removed the mask because he is tired of hiding his authenticity. Additionally, he's grown weary of having to be someone he isn't in order to please his partner. Maskless, he now begins a struggle to reclaim his authentic self. In his attempts to reclaim authenticity, he becomes challenging to deal with. The partner still wearing a mask is repulsed by this shift. This is where the struggles begin.

Avoid the challenges wearing a mask inevitably initiates by choosing to step into a relationship with your authentic self in full view. In many cases, people refrain from showing their true selves because they fear rejection. Showing your true self *can* lead to rejection; however, when you truly accept yourself and all your flaws, you will never fear rejection from others. The point is to love yourself first. When you love yourself, others will too. When you reject yourself, others will follow suit. Masks are unnecessary when you've discovered your inner light.

I had a client who struggled with masks in her relationship. Danielle wore a challenging mask. She was demanding, cold, and calculating. In the beginning of the relationship, she let Ryan know that she had very specific needs and expectations. Danielle demanded that she and Ryan go out a lot and travel together and that he provide her with a large amount of love. Ryan wore his own mask, the mask of a man who was accommodating and pleasing and who tried to give Danielle each and every thing she wanted. Ryan felt up to the task most of the time, but occasionally he didn't want to meet Danielle's demands. When he retreated and withdrew, Danielle and he would have big fights.

After several months of dating, Ryan took off his mask. Underneath, Ryan was frustrated because he felt he'd sacrificed his authenticity. Additionally, he was tired of pleasing a woman who appeared to never be happy about anything. Danielle was horrified by the removal of Ryan's mask. Their fights became more ferocious. A short while later, Danielle told Ryan she loved him. Soon afterwards, they broke up. Danielle was devastated by her loss. Ryan, while sad to no longer be with Danielle, was secretly relieved.

Did Danielle truly know the real Ryan? Did Ryan truly know the real Danielle? When Danielle and I worked together, we talked about her mask and Ryan's mask. She admitted that she had not been her authentic self with Ryan out of fear that he'd reject her. Underneath it all, Danielle felt she was too needy. She'd assumed that Ryan would not want a needy woman.

For nine months after they broke up, Danielle and Ryan fell into a pattern of texting each other. At times, the texting led them to bed. Their encounters proved to be frustrating for both parties. Danielle claimed the sex was amazing but felt that Ryan returned to his unmasked self immediately after he had an orgasm. Ryan, while very attracted to Danielle, found himself awkward in her presence. Ultimately, he'd choose to embrace his unmasked self, which upset Danielle. I explained to Danielle that sex was the only way Ryan could be authentic with her. When they weren't having sex, Ryan felt bitter. He was upset with himself for hiding his authenticity for such a long time. The bitterness that Ryan felt was partially projected at Danielle. He felt she made him hide behind his real self.

Danielle told me she never expected Ryan to behave a certain way. Unable to see her role in the dynamic, Danielle had a different perspective. Danielle saw the sexual encounters as an opportunity to reignite the relationship with Ryan. After having sex, she would bombard Ryan with prying questions about how he felt about her. And she'd ask if they could begin dating again. At that point, Ryan shut down. He resorted to silence. Not getting what she wanted, Danielle would get angry and swear off Ryan. She'd vent about her stupidity and how she was going to move on. Once the text messages started again, the next scenario played out in the same way. The cycle repeated for a year. In this situation, Danielle and Ryan's biggest lesson was to understand the power of being authentic. Ultimately, Danielle realized that she needed to address her own issues so she could heal and meet the right man.

We see Hollywood's version of this no-no in the 2009 movie *The Ugly Truth*. Katherine Heigl plays Abby, a producer for a failing morning show. Mike, played by Gerard Butler, hosts a dating show called *The Ugly Truth*. Through a series of coincidences, the evening before her station manager decides to offer Mike a segment on Abby's show, Abby tunes in to watch Mike's show. The manager is hoping for a much-needed ratings boost. In their first meeting Abby and Mike take an immediate dislike to each other, but they agree to work together for the benefit of the show. A short while later Abby meets Colin, the man of her dreams. Mike offers to assist her in landing him. The catch: Abby must follow Mike's advice, and only his advice. Abby agrees. As both Abby and Mike put their plan into action, we see the unsuspecting Colin begin to fall for Abby.

Mike's segment on Abby's show becomes so popular that he is offered a bigger gig for a nationwide competitor. Abby is sent on a business trip with Mike to convince him to stay with her network. To do so, Abby cancels her romantic weekend with Colin. After a successful appearance on the *Late, Late Show* with Craig Ferguson, Abby and Mike go out for drinks and dancing to celebrate. Abby tells Mike she would like him to stay so they can save the morning show. Mike admits he doesn't want to move out of the area because he wants to stay close to his family. In the elevator later, Mike kisses Abby. Mike and Abby are both confused about the kiss. Mike decides to go to his room, and Abby arrives at her room to find Colin waiting for her. Mike then decides to go to Abby's room, where he sees Colin surprising Abby. When Abby sees Mike, she realizes that Colin only likes the woman she has pretended to be, while Mike likes the real her. Abby breaks up with Colin and at the same time shows him how needy and naive she truly is. Mike is upset over losing Abby and leaves the morning show for another gig. The movie ends with Abby and Mike reuniting and expressing their feelings for each other.

Masks are easy to wear, but their effects can be detrimental to building the right relationship. Take the time to adjust your law of attraction as necessary in order to meet the right person. The time-table is up to you. The work is vital, if you commit to it.

KEY POINTS FOR REFLECTION AND JOURNALING

1. Do you have or have you had an expectation when starting a new relationship? Did this approach prove to be fruitful or disastrous?
2. Do you have specific needs which must be filled in a relationship? What do you do if your needs aren't being met? How do you feel about fulfilling your partner's needs?
3. What mask do you wear at the beginning of a relationship? How does this mask serve you?
4. What is your mask hiding? Can you make peace with your authentic self and show it to the world?
5. Which one of the no-nos would you find unpleasant in a partner? Is this a deal breaker or something you can work through?

A MEDITATION TO ASSIST THE JOURNEY

Find a quiet spot. Take several deep breaths. Focus on the breath going in and out of the body. Let go and release. Let go and release. Let go and release. Beginning with your toes and traveling up to the top of your head, slowly take the time to relax your body. Imagine all your stresses fading and floating away. Take several more deep breaths. When you are fully relaxed, see yourself sitting on a beautiful beach at sunset. Take another breath and allow yourself to go into a deeper place of relaxation. Just be. When you are ready, look around you.

See the red ball of the sun as it begins to sink below the horizon, smell the salty air, feel the sand between your toes and hear the waves as they lap gently onto the shore. Allow yourself to feel completely at peace here. Take a moment and connect with your heart. Go deep into the most beautiful cavern of your heart and allow yourself to feel the love there. What color do you see here? Is it gold? Is it green? Is it pink? Is it luminescent? Allow that love to spiral out of your heart and wash over you from head to toe. Feel this love resonating and vibrating all around you. Take several deep breaths. Reflect on your first encounter with an ex-boyfriend or ex-girlfriend. How did you feel after you met him or her? Excited? Nervous? Anxious? Curious? Happy? Surprised? How did meeting this person change your attitude or your approach to everything you did - go to work, go to school, interact with friends, interact with clients, run errands, workout, etc? Do you remember what was different about you? In many cases, your shift in attitude and behavior was due to the unknown. Fast-forward to six months into the relationship. What were your feelings at six months versus in the beginning of the relationship? In hindsight, did you have an expectation, wear a mask or expect needs to be fulfilled? Take a look at a specific occasion. What did you want in that situation? Did you get what you wanted? Would it have been easier to communicate your true desire? What did you learn from this experience? When you are ready, state the following aloud:

'I must be authentic in my communications. Being authentic means that I convey my desires to my partner with an open heart. I am aware that having expectations, wearing a mask and being needy is not an effective way to communicate. I see how these choices have affected who I am in a relationship. I do not make these choices anymore. I release this behavior for once and all. I reclaim the relationship of my dreams. I transform my energies. I shift my law of attraction qualities. I am in the proper alignment. I am grateful for the commitment I have made to myself as I walk this journey to the right relationship.'

When you are ready, return to the room and take notice of any sensations or feelings you are experiencing. If possible, take notes or record your impressions in a journal.

CHAPTER 11

CUTTING PSYCHIC CORDS

A psychic cord is an invisible cord that connects two individuals. There are several different types of psychic cords. The first are the cords we share with our parents. There are many stories of mothers who know their child is sick or injured from miles away, due to the cording that develops between children and their parents at the time of conception. The second type of psychic cord is the cords we share with friends, acquaintances, and coworkers. Depending on the nature of the relationship, these cords can be healthy and nurturing or unhealthy and toxic. The third type of psychic cord is the one we share with the men or women we date and have sex with. Similar to the second type of psychic cord, these cords can be positive, loving, and supportive or negative, debilitating, and detrimental.

On average, 97 percent of the population is unaware that psychic cording occurs when two people have sex. The two partners become linked together on many levels. They share similar thoughts, emotions, etc. Additionally, the cord provides the partners with the opportunity to share each other's energies. In a good relationship, the cord promotes unity between two parties who love and care for each other. One of my clairvoyant gifts includes the ability to perceive psychic cords. As a result of this, I have had the opportunity to see the cord between two parties who love each other. It is a beautiful sight. In a negative relationship, the cord acts as bondage. In this respect, one party is tied to the other without the ability to break free and move on. When a relationship ends, both parties should take action to cut the cord that connects them. Why?

- Cutting the cord stops the flow of energy between the two parties.
- Cutting the cord allows each party the opportunity to grieve the relationship and invite healing.
- Cutting the cord allows each party the opportunity to reclaim his or her own energies and become autonomous.

Many people are unwilling to do the work of cutting the cord after a relationship ends. Why? We live in a society that promotes quick gratification.

"Just got dumped?

Don't worry. There're more fish in the sea.

Get out to the bars, the clubs, or the gym. You'll meet someone in no time."

Society does not encourage us to take the time to reflect, review, and analyze a relationship that has ended. Post-relationship reflection is vital to move forward. Each party should take the time to evaluate his or her choices and mistakes. Taking the time for reflection is vital, in order to fully comprehend the teachings and/ or lessons of the relationship. While it is important for both parties to take a look at their choices, most people don't make the effort.

In a nutshell, we ignore the work. We opt to move on without any reflection whatsoever.

Several years ago, I became obsessed with educating people about psychic cords after experiences I'd had with two clients. A male client and a female client had individually come for readings. In the months leading up to the readings, both clients had ended relationships and had jumped into new relationships. My clients claimed that they were both happy in the beginning of the new relationships. However, after a few months, problems started creeping in. Suddenly, they were feeling the same level of unhappiness they had in their previous relationships. I knew what had happened. My first question to each of them was, "Did you cut the cord from the previous relationship?"

Blank looks and puzzled expression greeted the question. They didn't know what I was talking about. I explained to each of them what a psychic cord is, the importance of cutting a psychic cord, and the importance of healing in order to move on. My words fell on deaf ears. Astonishing to me, neither client wanted to do the work. Since my discussions with those two clients proved to be fruitless, I decided to educate people in a different way. I wrote a newsletter, posted it on my website, and sent it out to all my clients. I received some interesting responses. People were intrigued by what I'd said in the newsletter. However, in readings that followed, I heard the same responses as before. I couldn't believe it. I'd say to the client, "Did you read the newsletter about cutting psychic cords?"

The responses were the same.

"Yeah, I read it, but it sounds like a lot of work. I just want to meet the right person for me and be happy."

Ironically, everyone wants to meet that special someone, that soul mate, that person for them, but it seems no one wants to do the work necessary to arrive at the right place to meet that person. Are we lazy? Are we disinterested in learning from our past and our choices? Are we unable to see how the past affects the present? Are we too busy trying online or virtual dating? Why aren't we willing to do what it takes to make our lives better? I did not have an answer.

I decided I needed to pursue the issue in a new way. I approached the new age center where I did psychic readings and told them that I wanted to teach a workshop on cutting psychic cords. I explained that the experiential class would be part lecture, part meditation and said we'd actually do a cord cutting using candles and prayer. The director of programs told me that no one had ever taught a class like that before. She gave me a date. I signed a contract, and afterwards I asked Spirit to help me prepare for the workshop. I also asked for the right people to show up, people who would embrace cord cutting. I asked for people who really needed to make that shift in their lives.

The day before the workshop, six attendees had signed up. I had asked Spirit for a small group, and that is what was given to me. I felt that a small number of people would be important for making the change and bringing forth joy in their lives. Additionally, I understood the theory of six degrees of separation and knew that my attendees would tell others about their experiences, who would then tell others and then others.

The morning of the workshop, I trusted that everyone who showed up — people from different age groups and walks of life — needed to be there. As I looked around at the attendees, I admired their desire for better lives. At the end of the day, I told the group that I had been honored to facilitate the change in their lives. I added that I felt gratitude toward them for allowing me to assist them and explained that a new life had been born to each of them. In fact, their new lives had started the moment they'd decided to cut the cord.

In the weeks that followed, I received phone calls and e-mails from the attendees to bring me up to date on their new lives. The shifts had begun to occur. They were nervous and excited. They told their family and friends about the new start they'd been given. The word was spreading. Six months later, I found myself teaching the workshop again. However, it was different this time. I had changed, the curriculum had changed, and the people who were attracted to the class were more informed than my previous group. I attribute this to the law of attraction.

Several months earlier, the term *law of attraction* had presented itself to the new age community, and everyone was embracing it. How does the law of attraction tie into psychic cording? Because the law of attraction states that we are magnets, we continue to attract that which we vibrate or resonate. If we don't cut the cord from a previous lover or lovers, we will continue to attract the same "type" of personality into our lives. For example, if you are meeting men who habitually turn out to be abusive, it is because you haven't cut the cord from the first abusive man you met. Because the cord hasn't been cut, you keep attracting the same type of men. Similarly, if a man finds that he keeps meeting the same type of needy woman over and over, it is because he hasn't cut the cord from the first needy woman he was involved with.

By cutting the cord, incorporating our lessons, reviewing our choices, and allowing healing to occur, we change our vibration. When our vibration changes, we will meet different people. When we then open ourselves to meeting new people, we will ultimately embrace the right partner. Since my second group arrived with an understanding of like attracting like, it was easy for them to see and comprehend this concept. They came to my class to step out of the victim mode they'd been living in. Fired up about freeing themselves, they brought a dynamic, empowering energy to class.

When the cord-cutting process has been completed, the break is felt by both parties. For example, Party A, the initiator of the break, consciously recognizes that the cord has been cut, and he or she begins the healing process. Party B, the one the cord is being cut from, unconsciously notices within seven to ten days that something is different. In many cases, upon realizing that the cord has been cut, Party B will attempt to make contact. Why? Party B wants to reconnect to the energy of Party A. Party B likes how he or she feels when his or her energy is connected to Party A. He or she doesn't want to give up that energy. In many relationships, one party usually has stronger, vibrant, and more dynamic energy than the other. The party with the weaker, denser, and duller energy likes to be connected to the stronger energy. It makes them feel good. During this transition time, Party B may be vigilant.

When Party B pursues Party A to reconnect, he or she is behaving like a psychic vampire — individuals who surround themselves with people whose energies are strong, beautiful, and bright. They do this to feed off the good energies of others that make them feel good about themselves. Psychic vampires don't like their own energies, which are usually weak, ugly, and dark. They thrive upon sucking the energies from others, leaving them tired and depleted after being in their presence.

If Party A stays away from Party B, he or she will continue on the road to autonomy and healing. Party A needs to be strong and determined in order to move forward and heal completely. If Party A reunites with Party B, the energies will reconnect.

As you can see, cord cutting isn't only a psychic process. It is an emotional process. The biggest challenge in birthing a new life is the uncertainty of the unknown. In many cases, Party A is filled with the following thoughts: *Should I move forward? Will I be happy with a new life? Can I make it on my own? What is in store for me?*

Doubts present themselves. "Could I give her another chance? Will things will be different once I've cut the cord?" "Has he has changed since I've cut the cord? Do I owe it to him to give it another shot?"

For many clients, the struggle to move forward is coupled with uncertainties. The comfort of the familiar is often enticing enough to lead Party A to take steps backward and resume the relationship with Party B. I always advise clients to make the choice that they feel is in their best interest. There have been instances when a client cuts the cord, gets back with the ex, cuts the cord again, and then returns to the ex. This vicious cycle may be repeated over and over again until Party A realizes that nothing in the situation with Party B will change. At that point, the cord is cut one more — usually final — time.

A Hollywood example of cording can be found in the Jason Segal/Judd Apatow film, Forgetting Sarah Marshall. In the beginning of the movie, Sarah Marshall, played by Kristen Bell, breaks up with Peter Fretter, played by Jason Segal. Devastated by the breakup and unsure of how to move on, Peter begins sleeping around to get over Sarah. After one too many unsuccessful sexual trysts and lots of post-sex tears, Jason decides the only way he can get over Sarah is to take a vacation to Hawaii. Upon arriving at the resort that Sarah had bragged about, Peter is shocked to run into Sarah and her new love, Aldis, played by Russell Brand. Coincidence plays into the hand of fate when Peter's suite turns out to be next door to Sarah and Aldis's room. As luck would have it, Peter befriends Rachel, played by Mila Kunis, a sweet front-desk clerk with a bit of wild side. As Peter begins to feel better about himself and his blossoming relationship with Rachel, he finds out that Sarah cheated on him with Aldis for a year. Thrown by the news that Sarah was unfaithful for more than a year, Peter goes crazy while surfing and has an accident.

Later, during an uncomfortable dinner during which Sarah, Rachel, and Peter get drunk, Sarah begins to realize how improper and crass Aldis truly is. When Rachel and Peter have their first sexual encounter a few hours later, Sarah listens on the other side of the wall. In her attempt to make Peter jealous, Sarah has sex with Aldis and screams so loudly that Aldis get suspicious. A short while later, Sarah and Aldis argue and break up. After Aldis leaves the hotel to fly back to England, Peter goes to comfort Sarah. In between tears, Sarah admits to Peter that she is not over him and that she still loves him; she professes sorrow for breaking up with Peter. The two begin to fool around. Peter realizes something is wrong when he cannot get hard. After several attempts, Sarah asks Peter, "What is wrong with you?"

Peter declares, "Maybe the problem is that you broke my heart into a million pieces, and now my cock doesn't want to be around you anymore. Ever!" and he storms away.

In this example, it's clear that Peter didn't cut the cord with Sarah. Additionally, he didn't look at his or Sarah's choices in the relationship. He didn't take the time to mourn the relationship either. He jumped back into the dating pool by sleeping around to get over Sarah. It wasn't until he arrived in Hawaii and came face to face with Sarah that he began his healing process. Coincidentally when he had the opportunity to re-cord with Sarah, he couldn't. Why? He had already corded himself to Rachel, who had proved to be loving, caring, and supportive. Unconsciously, Peter knew that re-cording with Sarah would be a mistake. Peter knew that Sarah hadn't changed and that she only wanted him back because he had moved on to Rachel. Sarah, on the other hand, wanted to re-cord with Peter because she realized that she'd given up on a good man. Through his mourning process, Peter had shown himself to be the man she really wanted. Sadly, Sarah couldn't have Peter anymore because he'd developed strong affection for Rachel.

Sarah and Peter's story is similar to what happens in many relationships today. As you can see, cord cutting is vital. In order to meet the right person, we must reclaim ourselves and become whole again. Making the choice to cut old cords and heal to a level of wholeness puts us in a position of attracting a wonderful partner. The work takes commitment, but the end result is truly worth it.

KEY POINTS FOR REFLECTION AND JOURNALING

1. Do you know what a psychic cord is?
2. Are you aware of the lover or lovers that you are still corded with? Do you realize how this cording holds you back?
3. Have you been the psychic vampire in a relationship or has someone been feeding off you? How do you feel about that?
4. Are you committed to cutting your cord or cords in order to heal?
5. What does wholeness mean to you? Are you ready to be whole?

A MEDITATION TO ASSIST THE JOURNEY

Find a quiet spot. Take several deep breaths. Focus on the breath going in and out of the body. Let go and release. Let go and release. Let go and release. Beginning with your toes and traveling up to the top of your head, slowly take the time to relax your body. Imagine all your stresses fading and floating away. Take several more deep breaths. When you are fully relaxed, see yourself sitting on a beautiful beach at sunset. Take another breath and allow yourself to go into a deeper place of relaxation. Just be. When you are ready, look around you. See the red ball of the sun as it begins to sink below the horizon, smell the salty air, feel the sand between your toes and hear the waves as they lap gently onto the shore. Allow yourself to feel completely at peace here. Take a moment and connect with your heart. Go deep into the most beautiful cavern of your heart and allow yourself to feel the love there. What color do you see here? Is it gold? Is it green? Is it pink? Is it luminescent? Allow that love to spiral out of your heart and wash over you from head to toe. Feel this love resonating and vibrating all around you. Take several deep breaths. Be at peace. Allow yourself to go deeper and deeper. Ask to be shown a vision of the person to whom you need to cut the cord. Take a few moments to reflect on the relationship you have had with this person. What are/were the good dynamics of the relationship? What are/were the bad dynamics to the relationship? Is this person holding you back from the relationship of your dreams? If yes, can you find forgiveness for this person? Can you find forgiveness for yourself? Are you at peace with cutting the cord? When you are ready, state the following aloud:

'I am aware that there is an individual in my life whose presence, physical or psychic, prevents me from finding the relationship of my dreams. By staying connected to this individual, I am unable to grow and evolve. Today, I reclaim myself fully and completely. I choose to become whole. I cut the cord from this person. I cut the cord from this person. I cut the cord from this person. I reclaim the relationship of my dreams. I transform my energies. I shift my law of attraction qualities. I am in the proper alignment. I am grateful for the commitment I have made to myself as I walk this journey to the right relationship.'

When you are ready, return to the room and take notice of any sensations or feelings you are experiencing. If possible, take notes or record your impressions in a journal.

CHAPTER 12

TO HEAL OR NOT TO HEAL

What is healing? Healing is the process by which we acknowledge, release, and forgive those aspects of ourselves that must die in order for us to move forward. Why is it important to embrace healing as part of our journey? When those aspects die, we allow more light to fill our beings. When more light fills our bodies, we become more aligned with Spirit. Through this process, we experience rebirth.

I've been asked a countless number of times about the process of healing and why it should be pursued. Healing work is vital to the evolution of our souls. Most people think that they've come to planet Earth to fall in love, have children, raise a family, and provide for themselves and their family. While that is true to a certain extent, we actually come to planet Earth to grow on a soul level. The purpose of the soul reincarnating over and over is to further develop our evolution. It is possible to grow by learning what it is like to be part of a relationship, to raise a child, to learn a trade or career, to express ourselves creatively, to set goals, to achieve those goals, and to take care of ourselves. But our sole purpose is to work through our karma by learning lessons, teaching others, and allowing our souls to blossom like beautiful flowers. However, many people are disconnected from the soul's journey.

Why should we care about the evolution of our soul? Our biggest achievements aren't about how much money we make, how popular we are, or how many toys we have. Our biggest achievement is to find our way back to and become one with Spirit. When we focus on the soul's growth, becoming one with Spirit becomes possible.

When the concept of the law of attraction was introduced several years ago, many individuals could not recognize the way the law tied into the soul's growth. Today, we have a better understanding of the simple yet complex concept of like attracting like. The law of attraction plays an important role in healing because it sends to us exactly what we vibrate. Often we aren't aware of what we are vibrating. If we vibrate fear, we get more fear. If we vibrate anger, we get more anger. If we vibrate poverty, we get more poverty. When we have a deeper understanding of what we are vibrating, we can embrace healing. Healing allows us the opportunity to change what we are both conscious of and unconscious of. Those of us who do the work, do the healing, and remove the darkness within change our law of attraction. By doing this work, we ultimately attract to ourselves the soul mate or job that is the best fit for us.

If we don't do the work of healing ourselves, we will continue to meet men or women, and we'll still find a job, but usually both scenarios will mirror the unfinished business we've yet to deal with. Healing work is vital because the process allows us to create an awesome life for ourselves.

How do we go about healing ourselves? There are many different ways to embrace healing. Traditional forms of healing involve working with a priest or minister or going to psychotherapy. Over time, these methods have proven effective in allowing people to gain perspective on the events that have shaped their lives, find forgiveness and release, and ultimately move forward. Some nontraditional or new age forms of healing include Reiki, healing touch, Barbara Brennan technique, pranic healing, massage, Rolfing, shamanism, yoga, rebirthing, and cranial sacral therapy. For a client who wants to dip their toe in the ocean of healing, I recommend a Reiki session as a good starting point because a Reiki session allows for subtle energetic shifts to occur. The energy of Reiki is warm, inviting, and relaxing. Many clients fall asleep during a session due to the peaceful nature of the energy.

Whether you are looking for a Reiki master, a cranial sacral therapist, or a Rolfer, how do you go about finding the right healer for yourself? Here are some suggestions.

- Visit new age stores and ask if they recommend any healers or whether they have any staff members who give healing sessions on- or offsite.
- Visit new age stores to see if they carry any new age magazines. If so, review the magazines for articles or ads posted by healers.
- Attend new age lectures, classes, or workshops and ask about healers who use the same space or are part of their teaching faculty.
- Attend new age or psychic fairs for a fifteen-minute session with at least one healer.
- Visit new age centers and inquire about healer's studios that are held onsite. A healer's studio is a night dedicated to healing; a client can receive several types of healing sessions from various healers at a discounted price.

- When looking for a healer who specializes in Barbara Brennan technique, pranic healing, Rolfing, or cranial sacral therapy, do Google searches for the organizations that certify these healers. Most certifying institutions will have an option on their website that helps you locate a practitioner in your area.
- Ask friends or classmates where they found their healer and whom they work with.
- Some day spas and massage centers have healers on staff who provide cranial, Rolfing, or Barbara Brennan techniques. Check out their websites or inquire in person.

Once you've completed your research and have experienced a few mini-sessions with some healers or attended a healer's studio, it is time to establish a working relationship with one healer who will assist you on your journey. The next step is to conduct interviews to determine who is the best healer for your needs. Here is a list of questions to ask.

- What training have they received for their particular modality and have they received any certification?
- What is the scope of the work performed in the healing session(s), and how long does a session last? What is the format of each session?
- When are sessions held? Every week? Once every two weeks? At the determination of the client?
- Does the client need to commit to a series of sessions? Can the client take a break or stop sessions when he or she wants?
- Where do the sessions take place? What should be brought to the sessions? What clothes are appropriate for the work of the session?

- Does the healer offer a trial session or one-time session? If yes, what is the cost?
- What is the cost of a regular session? Is there a discount for blocks of five, ten, or fifteen sessions paid in advance?
- What responsibilities does the healer assume for the session(s)?
- What responsibilities does the client assume for the session(s)?
- After session(s), should the patient keep a journal or engage in any other activity that will assist the healing process?

In most cases, a commitment of two sessions monthly is an effective way to begin the release process. Over time, many individuals find they are more calm, focused, and relaxed — less stressed and more grounded.

When we address unfinished issues regarding our parents, relationship disappointments, career decisions, and issues of health and self-care, we allow those old parts of ourselves to slip away. Healing assists us in releasing illusions about who we are, what our lives are meant to be, where we are supposed to be at what time in our lives, how we should live our lives, and our expectations about life.

For clients who want to become a healer, I recommend that a Reiki I course. Usui Reiki was created in Japan. While the exact origination of this healing methodology is not completely known, Reiki is often referred to as the "universal life force." Reiki I students are attuned, or given this energy, by a Reiki master, an individual who has completed all the levels of Reiki training and has committed to sharing Reiki with the world by teaching Reiki, passing along attunements, and performing healings. In addition to learning the history and the origination of Reiki, students are taught the hand positions for self-healing. After receiving the Reiki I energy, students are encouraged to do self-sessions in order to allow the energy to become stronger. After receiving a Reiki I attunement, the student will begin a cleansing, or clearing, process. This gradual release of old energies allows students to let go of those parts and pieces of themselves that no longer serve their highest purpose. Reiki energy is unique because it has an intelligence of its own. The wisdom of the Reiki energy is amazing, because it goes exactly where it is needed. Unlike other healing modalities, where energy is directed to specific chakras, levels of the aura, or areas of the body, the Reiki I practitioner does not need to be aware of any issue or issues being addressed. The practitioner merely opens up to the energy, lays the hands on (or above, if contact is not desired) the client, and allows for its flow. Because Reiki is not tied to any specific religion or religious group, I find it is a great starting point for clients of all backgrounds. When I was first attuned to Reiki I energy, I immediately fell in love with the heat I felt in my hands. Initially I followed the traditional Reiki hand placements for the giving of a self-session, but I found in time that my hands intuitively went where they needed to go.

Because Reiki is so widely used all over the world today, you can locate teachers quite easily. Reiki is simple; it allows an individual to get started on the path to healing with ease and freedom. Down the road, the student can choose to become attuned to Reiki II and Reiki III and ultimately become a Reiki master, if he or she chooses. The benefit of additional training and Reiki attunements allow for increased ability to bring forth more energy. The higher levels of Reiki allow students to learn how to conduct sessions for others and to send Reiki long distance. Additional attunements call for deeper release work, and this allows the student to embrace more light in their lives.

For individuals who shy away from working with or becoming a healer, becoming more in tune with the body to increase body consciousness, as well as feelings of being centered and grounded, is a viable option. In these circumstances, I suggest a yoga class. Yoga has the ability to unite body, mind, and spirit. This union allows us the opportunity to feel safe within our bodies and learn how to properly nurture ourselves. Yoga teaches us to trust the inherent wisdom found deep within our bodies and to connect with ourselves in a deeper manner. Another benefit of yoga is that it will ultimately allow connection with the various chakra centers of our body. When we connect with these centers, healing can begin.

There will always be people who claim that they do not have the time, energy, or focus to address their healing. I often wonder if fear of change or fear of becoming someone new holds such individuals back. Over time, I've seen a refusal to heal lead to the feeling of being stuck and ultimately to depression. Once depression sets in and life spirals downward, it is even harder to embrace healing.

We are fortunate because Spirit allows us free will. Free will enables us to embrace healing or deny it. Ultimately, the road to a happier life comes when we embrace the journey our soul has set out for us. In embracing the journey, we heal. In healing, we allow more light to fill us. In allowing the light to become one with us, we find our way home.

KEY POINTS FOR REFLECTION AND JOURNALING

1. What does the term *healing* mean to you?
2. Do you understand the importance of the soul's evolution?
3. Can you understand the correlation between law of attraction and healing?
4. Would you consider engaging in healing sessions to assist you in your journey?
5. If you could heal one thing about yourself, what would it be? Once healed, how would your life be different?

A MEDITATION TO ASSIST THE JOURNEY

Find a quiet spot. Take several deep breaths. Focus on the breath going in and out of the body. Let go and release. Let go and release. Let go and release. Beginning with your toes and traveling up to the top of your head, slowly take the time to relax your body. Imagine all your stresses fading and floating away. Take several more deep breaths. When you are fully relaxed, see yourself sitting on a beautiful beach at sunset. Take another breath and allow yourself to go into a deeper place of relaxation. Just be. When you are ready, look around you. See the red ball of the sun as it begins to sink below the horizon, smell the salty air, feel the sand between your toes and hear the waves as they lap gently onto the shore. Allow yourself to feel completely at peace here. Take a moment and connect with your heart. Go deep into the most beautiful cavern of your heart and allow yourself to feel the love there. What color do you see here? Is it gold? Is it green? Is it pink? Is it luminescent? Allow that love to spiral out of your heart and wash over you from head to toe. Feel this love resonating and vibrating all around you. Take several deep breaths. Be at peace. Allow yourself to go deeper and deeper. Allow the events of your life to pass through your mind. Recall all the beautiful, amazing and loving memories in addition to the unpleasant, sad or confusing memories. Do you see or recall any experiences that need healing? Are you ready to embrace healing? Are you ready to make your life better? Can you make a commitment to yourself? When you are ready, state the following aloud:

'I am aware of an unpleasant experience(s) that need to be healed. As long as I choose to ignore the importance of healing, I am prohibited from having the relationship of my dreams.

Today, I reclaim myself fully and completely. I choose whole-ness. I choose healing. I reclaim the relationship of my dreams. I transform my energies. I shift my law of attraction qualities. I am in the proper alignment. I am grateful for the commit-ment I have made to myself as I walk this journey to the right relationship.'

When you are ready, return to the room and take notice of any sensations or feelings you are experiencing. If possible, take notes or record your impressions in a journal.

PART III:
FINDING THE RIGHT RELATIONSHIP

CHAPTER 13

THE CART GOES BEFORE
THE HORSE

Recently a friend of a friend referred a new client to me. When we finally connected, this client decided to set up a phone reading. On the appointed date and time, she called, and we began our session. As is the case with all readings, I had pulled some tarot cards from my deck and immediately started to convey the information I was getting from Spirit. While in the middle of a sentence about how I saw her switching jobs and taking on the responsibility for managing a large group of people, she rudely cut me off. She indicated that she wasn't interested in hearing about a job change but instead wanted to know when she'd meet her future husband. I explained that she wasn't ready to meet him yet but that I could see him coming in eighteen to twenty-four months. At that point, she asked for specifics. Where would they meet? What would he be wearing?

How would they meet? What was his first initial? What did he do for work? Et cetera.

She explained that many years earlier a psychic had given such specifics to her mom, indicating how she'd meet her dad. At some point, her mom did meet her dad in the way the psychic had predicted. This client wanted me to provide the same type of information to her. I told her that all psychics work differently and that the reason I didn't work that way was because it puts people in a "push" mode versus an "allowance" mode. She asked me what a push mode was. A push mode occurs after we get information from a reading about someone or something that is supposed to happen in our lives, and instead of allowing it to happen in its natural order, we *push* to make it happen sooner. Allowance mode is when we get information from a reading and *allow* it to be a small seed that is planted in the back of our mind.

When divine timing occurs and the moment is right, the opportunity or opportunities present themselves. Sadly, a majority of us like to live in push mode all the time. We want to meet Mr. or Ms. Right according to our own timing instead of when we are truly ready for them to arrive in our lives. In many cases, this behavior is not limited to relationships. We do this in our careers as well. We are never comfortable with the ground we stand upon because we are always striving to be elsewhere. We want to be in that space or place that is six, nine, twelve, eighteen, or twenty-four months in the future. We know that we will be happier in that place than in the present. Because of this, we ignore today; we ignore the present moment. While we may not be happy with the present moment, it is the place where we have power.

Our power comes from this moment and this choice. In the present moment, we can choose to be happy and joyful or sad and unfulfilled. Our decision to be happy and joyful in the present comes when we are at peace with Spirit's plan for our life. Our decision to be sad and unfulfilled comes when we feel we need to have future events arrive in our life today, instead of waiting for events to unfold as they should. When we are in push mode, we discount the plan that Spirit has for us and put our plan first. I call this putting the cart before the horse. When the cart is behind the horse, we believe that Spirit will make things happen for us as they are meant to occur. If more of us believed in the cart going *behind* the horse, we'd save ourselves a lot of frustration and aggravation.

Also, push mode drains our energy. In this mode, we exert a tremendous amount of life force because we are working in opposition to allowance mode, putting forth effort due to lack of faith. Over time, this constant pushing is exhausting. Similar to the fish that gets confused and tries to swim against the current, we choose to battle against the flow of life. The poor fish that is exerting all his efforts in swimming upstream watches in frustration as the other fish gladly ride the current downstream. The fish that ride the current downstream are in tune with Spirit's plan for their greatest and highest good. They believe that all the wonderful things they desire will happen to them in accordance with divine timing. Additionally, they are also connected with their divine will and trust their higher selves to watch over their life plan.

A final note about push mode is that it gives us a sense of control. Push mode allows us to feel like we are in charge of our lives. Society conditions us that we need to be in control of our life in order to manage it properly. We are so busy controlling that we leave no space to relinquish. Push mode is the ego voicing its opinion by putting itself and its needs before Spirit.

When did our faith in ego become stronger than our faith in Spirit? Why did we lose our faith in Spirit? Our human nature, our society, and our cultural conditioning have taught us to go after what we want. We are programmed to push for the best grades, the best schools, the best teachers, the best training, the best car, the best clothes, the best computer, the best cell phone, the best man, and the best woman. Advertising and marketing campaigns plague us with the ideology of having it all — now. Thus, we are surrounded with the dynamic that feeds our ego the most: greed. The space, or allowance, for Spirit's plan doesn't fit in with corporate culture; nor would it sell many products.

Allowance mode is your acknowledgement to ego and to Spirit that you are willing to wait for the right partner to appear in your life. Allowance mode is about having blind faith that Spirit will subtly guide you to the perfect space and place to meet that special someone. When the divine timing is right and when the stars are aligned as they need to be, he or she will appear as destined.

Allowance mode is not exhausting. Allowance mode is not demanding, and, more importantly, allowance mode will not leave you feeling depleted and empty. As a society, we don't have a lot of patience for allowance mode, but isn't it important to have patience for Spirit? Allowance mode reaffirms your connection to Spirit and allows it to grow stronger. Allowance mode puts you in a position of saying "I trust you" to Spirit.

Once we make the commitment to allowance mode, we become liberated, free to joyously live with the knowledge that Spirit will provide for us in accordance with divine will and divine timing. We believe that Mr. or Ms. Right will appear as they are destined to. We can never go wrong by putting ourselves into allowance mode. Our decision to put our trust in Spirit can lead to an amazing amount of joy, if we embrace it.

My client became more agitated when I told her that she needed to be alone right now and to continue to work through the unresolved issues from her divorce. She remarked that she was going to a shrink for that kind of work and didn't see the need to address it on her own. I explained to her that while I believed in the benefits of psychotherapy to assist her in intellectual healing, she needed energetic healing to assist her on the physical level. I suggested deep tissue massage or a form of energetic healing, like Reiki or healing touch. My client was not open to the idea and persisted in asking me questions about her new love. I explained to her that she had not met her new love at this time. I added that she'd meet him through an introduction in about eighteen to twenty-four months. I told her he was a business professional who had been divorced a few years earlier.

I further explained that the timetable was up to her. I told her that a decision to commit to working on herself could speed up the process of meeting him. I added that she also had the option of doing nothing; she'd meet him according to Spirit at the appropriate time. Instead of feeling as though she now had a plan, my client told me she felt challenged by what I'd said. She was the classic case of someone who wanted to be in charge of her destiny but wouldn't take responsibility for healing herself or her wounds. Instead of agreeing that she wasn't ready to meet Mr. Right, she continued to say she felt her timing was perfect. Because her ego was voicing its opinion loudly, she couldn't hear the truth I was expressing. In her mind, she wanted to control when she'd meet Mr. Right and at the same time look away from the unfinished business from her previous relationship. I explained to her the importance of the law of attraction and the need to make peace with her past. She wasn't interested in what I had to say.

After I got off the phone with the client, I was once again reminded of how challenging our lives can be when we don't have a good, strong, viable connection with Spirit. Having a strong connection with Spirit allows us to put our faith in divine timing. If my client had had a strong faith in Spirit, she'd know that Mr. Right would pop up as he needed to for her greatest and highest good. If I had given this client the answers she wanted — his name starts with an R, he'll be wearing a green tie, and you'll meet him at a birthday party — my client would have made it her business to attend every birthday party possible in the next eighteen to twenty-four months to seek out Mr. R with the green tie. This is classic push mode.

Several months later, another client came to me for a reading. At the beginning of the session, she inquired about when she'd meet someone new. I told her I saw her meeting someone through some type of work-related function. I described the man she'd meet and talked briefly about his personality and attributes. I also told her that upon meeting him she'd think little of the introduction or the moments she'd spend talking to him. In other words, there would be no cupid's arrow piercing her heart, nor would she be struck by lightning upon meeting him. I cautioned her to let the process unfold in the way it needed to.

Several months passed before the client contacted me for another reading. As soon as the session began, she detailed every corporate event, meeting, cocktail party, and interoffice encounter she'd had. She told me about the four or five new men she'd met, but she indicated that there were no fireworks. I reminded her that the initial meeting with this man would have been brief and almost unimportant to her. She asked me if she'd met the man she was supposed to meet. I told her yes. She then proceeded to describe in detail each man she'd met: name, title, personality, and physical description. She wanted to know if any of the men she'd described were her new lover. I told her he was not amongst any of the men she'd described because her encounter with her prospective lover had been forgettable. I explained that the encounter had occurred the way it was supposed to. I explained to her that she would meet this man again when the timing was right.

This news created more anxiety for her; she sat across from me, trying to remember someone she'd forgotten. In time, my client gave up trying to remember her forgettable experience with the stranger. As fate would have it, their paths crossed again about six months later. In a different space and in a different place, my client welcomed the opportunity to embrace this new lover into her life. As of my last conversation with this client, they were still together.

KEY POINTS FOR REFLECTION AND JOURNALING

1. Do you understand the concept of putting the cart before the horse?
2. Do you understand what push mode is?
3. Can you see instances in your life where you've operated in push mode?
4. Do you understand what allowance mode is?
5. Are you willing to do the work that is necessary to put yourself in alignment for the right partner? If yes, can you wait for divine timing?

A MEDITATION TO ASSIST THE JOURNEY

Find a quiet spot. Take several deep breaths. Focus on the breath going in and out of the body. Let go and release. Let go and release. Let go and release. Beginning with your toes and traveling up to the top of your head, slowly take the time to relax your body. Imagine all your stresses fading and floating away. Take several more deep breaths. When you are fully relaxed, see yourself sitting on a beautiful beach at sunset. Take another breath and allow yourself to go into a deeper place of relaxation. Just be. When you are ready, look around you. See the red ball of the sun as it begins to sink below the horizon, smell the salty air, feel the sand between your toes and hear the waves as they lap gently onto the shore. Allow yourself to feel completely at peace here. Take a moment and connect with your heart. Go deep into the most beautiful cavern of your heart and allow yourself to feel the love there. What color do you see here? Is it gold? Is it green? Is it pink? Is it luminescent? Allow that love to spiral out of your heart and wash over you from head to toe. Feel this love resonating and vibrating all around you. Take several deep breaths. Take a moment to be completely at peace. Allow yourself to go deeper and deeper. Reflect on the events in your life. Do you see examples of push mode? Do you feel or have you felt that you must manage all aspects of your life in order to fulfill your desires? What was the outcome of those events or experiences where you pushed? Do you see how spiritual guidance could have assisted you? Do you see examples of allowance mode? If yes, how did those events turn out? When you are ready state the following:

'I am aware that I operate from push mode. I see that this way of conducting my life is not effective. My decision to ignore allowance mode results in events or experiences ending in a less than desirable outcome. I have been blocked from the relationship of my dreams. Today, I put my faith in Spirit. I put my faith in the divine plan. I know that my commitment to the journey will allow me to reclaim myself fully and completely. I reclaim the relationship of my dreams. I transform my energies. I shift my law of attraction qualities. I am in the proper alignment. I am grateful for the commitment I have made to myself as I walk this journey to the right relationship.'

When you are ready, return to the room and take notice of any sensations or feelings you are experiencing. If possible, take notes or record your impressions in a journal.

CHAPTER 14

C-O-M-M-I-T-M-E-N-T

If you ask a hundred people what the term *commitment* means, you'll likely get a hundred different answers. Our affection or dislike for the word *commitment* goes back to what we perceived about our parents' commitment, or lack thereof, to each other. When we look at the word *commitment* relative to our parents' and grandparents' generations, the word often meant "till death do us part."Those vows also included "in sickness and in health, for richer or poorer, and for better or worse." Some people define *commitment* as refraining from seeing, dating, or sleeping with anyone else. For others, commitment means the promise of a ring with the promise of marriage and children. For others, commitment is a long noose tied around the neck, limiting freedom.

In the last thirty years, the divorce rate of 50 percent and the ease in which a marriage can be ended have led to differing attitudes about commitment. While couples do commit to each other today, the commitment is different. We live in a different world, one that enables us to approach commitment with less of a focus on *forever* and more of a focus on *right now*. Why has this approach come about? If you are the son or daughter of divorced parents, you are acutely aware of the affects and effects of a broken marriage. Similarly, if you were raised in a single-parent home and never knew your other parent, you will view commitment differently. To you, commitment means taking full responsibility for raising a child, making ends meet on your own, and making sacrifices you never dreamed of making.

If you were fortunate enough to be raised by both parents, you view commitment as two parties coming together in a union. This union comprises the combining of two lives, agreeing to love and support each other financially and emotionally, raising children, willingly providing emotional and financial support for your children, and preparing for retirement. It is obvious that the perception of marriage and commitment from a child who was raised by both parents varies from that of peers raised by divorced parents.

Many years ago the term *commitment* included the assumption of specific roles. Men were the providers and pursued careers outside of the home, while women raised children and maintained the home. Many women have not assumed traditional roles since the 1960s. Today's women may want careers in addition to marriage and children, and today's men may want a woman who will provide for their needs but who are also willing to raise children. With these differing assumptions, it is easy to see how coming to a place of commitment, that middle ground between two people, becomes harder and harder. As evident in movies, media, and politics, couples are finding that they need to write their own commitment rules.

Robert and Samantha had been together for three and a half years. Samantha was getting ready for a bigger commitment to

Robert, but she was concerned about falling off the partner track at her firm. She felt she'd put time, money, and energy into her career and could not risk losing ground by settling into marriage with Robert. Robert, on the other hand, felt it was time that he and Samantha moved forward. He was a successful engineer who'd recently completed his master's degree. To him, the next natural step would be for him and Samantha to get engaged. Samantha told me that she wanted a long engagement that lasted two or two and half years; Robert didn't want to wait that long. He wanted them to marry in less than a year.

I recognized that their differences in commitment came from the different levels of commitment experienced during their upbringing. I asked both Robert and Samantha to examine their underlying attitudes about commitment. Robert explained that he'd come from a traditional household, which included a stay-at-home mom. Once married, he wanted Samantha to cut back on work and her long billable hours so they could focus on having children. Raised by a single parent and watching her mother struggle to make ends meet, Samantha, knowing her partnership track would be sacrificed, couldn't bear the thought of reducing her hours. Samantha felt that having a career was the important key to being able to provide financial support. Obviously, Robert and Samantha were at a crossroads in their relationship.

It was apparent that both Robert and Samantha had very different versions of what commitment meant. As a result of this, I encouraged them to try and find common ground. After several sessions, Robert and Samantha agreed to wait six months before getting engaged. Once engaged, they would commit to marrying within a year. Robert and Samantha agreed to hold off on plans to have children for six months. This six-month period allows Samantha the opportunity to see if she will be voted a partner. Once that process was completed, they would begin trying to have a baby. The compromise allowed both Robert and Samantha to get what they wanted. More importantly, both Robert and Samantha were able to find peace in their respective levels of commitment.

Interestingly, not all commitments lead to marriage. Goldie Hawn and Kurt Russell have been together for over fifteen years without marrying. Together the two of them raised Goldie's children from her first marriage, Kate and Oliver Hudson. For Goldie and Kurt, a commitment to be with each other, love each other, and be devoted to each other came without a wedding. Similarly, Brad Pitt and Angelina Jolie have committed to each other and the raising of seven children, some of whom are adopted and some who are their own children. This modern couple opted not to marry but have remained committed to each other despite huge Hollywood careers, Academy Award nominations, and their tireless work for charities all over the world.

How does a couple get to that place of commitment? Is it natural to commit to someone after spending two or three years together? For a man, is this the next logical step? In the 2010 movie *He's Just Not That Into You*, Ben, played by Bradley Cooper, tells Anna, played by Scarlett Johansson, that he married his wife, Janine, played by Jennifer Connolly, because they'd been together for several years and it was "the next thing to do." He adds that he married Janine because she gave him an ultimatum. In a later scene, we see Ben and Neil, played by Ben Affleck, out on Neil's sailboat. Neil is upset because Beth, played by Jennifer Aniston, has recently broken up with him. The breakup came after Neil announced he never wanted to marry. In a discussion about commitment and marriage, Ben explains to Neil that no man really wants to get married because he'll think about all the women he's "missing out on." Neil is surprised by this revelation because he only wants to be with Beth.

A short while later, Beth's father has a heart attack at her sister's wedding. While taking care of her ill father, Beth is shocked to notice her sisters' spouses' lack of commitment toward their wives, and she realizes that her relationship with Neil was more like a marriage than her sisters' marriages. At her parent's house, Neil surprises Beth by pitching in to help out during her father's recovery. This leads to the couples' reconciliation. Shortly after their reconciliation, Neil proposes to Beth and tells her he wants her to be happy and knows that marrying him will make her happy. This movie accurately portrays the differing approaches to commitment that are so prevalent in today's society.

I was fortunate to be exposed to today's attitudes toward commitment during a previous job. Several years ago I was employed as a dance instructor. I taught group classes and private lessons, and a big percentage of the people I taught were wedding couples. In the days and weeks leading up to the wedding, dance instruction was one of the last few things to be checked off prospective brides' lists. After discussing their song selection on the phone and finding the music on CD, I would begin the choreography for their bridal dance. My first meeting with each couple included teaching them the beginning portions of their wedding dance. In these first few moments with each couple, I would immediately get a sense of their commitment to each other and to their upcoming nuptials. I could easily tell which couples who would make it and which couples would not. Working with these couples included hearing stories about the details of the wedding: who was attending, who was walking with whom, who chose the wedding song, how the couple had met, how long they'd been together, whether parents were going to be at the wedding or were deceased, and whether or not the bride was happy with everything. I gained a huge insight into the commitment they shared.

Was the groom there and meeting her halfway on all the details, or was he merely showing up to do his part? I remember a prospective groom who told me that he felt his wedding dance was a joke.

I had just demonstrated the choreography I had created for their dance to "At Last …" by Etta James. I was surprised by his response and on the verge of saying something when the bride jumped to my defense. After several moments, the couple began arguing. I told the two of them I'd step out of the studio to give them some time alone. I watched from the reception desk as the couple continued arguing for several minutes. Finally, I saw things settle down. When I reentered the room, we resumed learning the choreography as if nothing had been said to me. Two weeks later and apparently happier with the dance choreography, the groom told me he loved the dance and admitted his previous outburst had nothing to do with me. I knew that. I also knew that taking a stand and learning how to lead his wife in their wedding dance was the final step he needed to take toward committing to his future. The wedding and their dance were beautiful.

KEY POINTS FOR REFLECTION AND JOURNALING

1. What does commitment mean to you?
2. How has your parents' commitment to each other or lack thereof affected your ideas about commitment?
3. Has your definition of commitment changed in the last five years? If yes, what is the catalyst for this change? Do you think your definition will change again? Why?
4. Take a moment to think about a previous relationship. How did you and your partner view commitment? Were there a lot of similarities? Were there a lot of differences?
5. If you meet the right partner, are you willing to find a common ground with him or her in order to find the right commitment level for the two of you?

A MEDITATION TO ASSIST THE JOURNEY

Find a quiet spot. Take several deep breaths. Focus on the breath going in and out of the body. Let go and release. Let go and release. Let go and release. Beginning with your toes and traveling up to the top of your head, slowly take the time to relax your body. Imagine all your stresses fading and floating away. Take several more deep breaths. When you are fully relaxed, see yourself sitting on a beautiful beach at sunset. Take another breath and allow yourself to go into a deeper place of relaxation. Just be. When you are ready, look around you. See the red ball of the sun as it begins to sink below the horizon, smell the salty air, feel the sand between your toes and hear the waves as they lap gently onto the shore. Allow yourself to feel completely at peace here. Take a moment and connect with your heart. Go deep into the most beautiful cavern of your heart and allow yourself to feel the love there. What color do you see here? Is it gold? Is it green? Is it pink? Is it luminescent? Allow that love to spiral out of your heart and wash over you from head to toe. Feel this love resonating and vibrating all around you. Take several deep breaths. Take a moment to be completely at peace. Allow yourself to go deeper and deeper. Connect with your definition of commitment. What shaped your view of commitment? Your upbringing? Your relationship with your parents? Was it something else? Do you feel that you could shift or change your definition of commitment? If no, why not? Does commitment have to be on your terms? If you were going to lose your relationship because of your unwillingness to shift your view of commitment, how would you respond? When you are ready state the following:

'I have a particular view of commitment and the role I want it to play in the relationship of my dreams. In my desire to put myself in the right alignment for this relationship, I commit to being flexible in finding a level of commitment that works for both of us. I reclaim the relationship of my dreams. I transform my energies. I shift my law of attraction qualities. I am in the proper alignment. I am grateful for the commitment I have made to myself as I walk this journey to the right relationship.'

When you are ready, return to the room and take notice of any sensations or feelings you are experiencing. If possible, take notes or record your impressions in a journal.

CHAPTER 15

THERE'S AN ELEPHANT
IN THE ROOM

Boy meets Girl. Boy chats with Girl. Boy is cautious with his words while speaking to Girl. Boy is trying to see if Girl is interested. Girl is distracted. Girl doesn't really think much of the conversation. Girl is at work and busy with what she's doing. Boy leaves. Girl realizes after the fact that Boy was interested. As Boy walks away, he doesn't know what to think of Girl. Was she interested or just being nice? Girl thinks about the conversation with Boy. Girl realizes she was rude. Girl decides she needs to be more available next time. Boy and Girl meet again. Boy chats with Girl. Girl is more attentive this time, and Boy and Girl have a nice chat. Boy leaves thinking Girl is interested. Boy decides he will ask Girl out on a date the next time he sees her. Girl feels better about this encounter with Boy. She hopes he'll ask her out.

A week later, Boy and Girl meet for dinner. Boy is nervous. Girl is nervous. Boy talks a lot. Boy tells Girl everything about his life — who he is, what he's about, how he was raised, what his morals, values, and beliefs are. Girl is surprised by Boy's openness and honesty. Girl is so nervous that she doesn't say a lot. Girl talks about some basics in her life but doesn't reveal too much. Girl has a good time on the date. Boy has a good time on the date. Boy and Girl trade text messages the day after the date.

A week goes by, and Girl has not heard from Boy. Girl begins to wonder if something went wrong and calls me for a psychic reading. After explaining her story to me, Girl asks what went wrong. I explain to Girl that Boy has approval and acceptance issues. I tell Girl that Boy's revelation of who he is, what he's about, how he was raised, etc., was Boy's way of "putting all the cards on the table." Boy was unconsciously asking for acceptance and approval from Girl. Girl told me she could relate to some of Boy's life, but not all of it. Girl tells me that she enjoyed Boy's honesty but was overwhelmed when Boy dumped his life story upon her. Girl said she'd hope that the first date would be about getting to know the basics of each others' lives and determining if there was more to discover. Boy had an expectation. Boy was looking for Girl to stroke his ego. Girl didn't meet that expectation. Because Girl didn't give Boy what he needed, Boy has backed out. Girl is angry. Girl is hurt. Boy is angry. Boy is frustrated.

I tell Girl not to call Boy. I tell Girl that Boy will call in five to seven days. I ask Girl if she can tolerate the "white elephant." Girl asks what a white elephant is. I explain that the white elephant is Boy's issue — his need for approval from outside sources. I ask Girl if the white elephant is a deal breaker or something she can live with. While Girl is pondering my question, I explain to her that the white elephant will remain between Boy and Girl until the issue is resolved. I add that Boy will continue to have this issue until he finds acceptance and approval for whatever part of his story he's uncomfortable with. I add that Girl has her own white elephant, but Boy hasn't seen it yet. Girl asks me what I am talking about.

I ask Girl why she was so nervous about this date. Girl explains that she isn't thrilled about her upbringing, her relationship with her parents, or her choice of a career. When I ask her what is wrong with her career, Girl balks and begins making excuses. I ask Girl if she is looking for approval somewhere in her own life story. Girl thinks a moment and then realizes that she has a white elephant too. Girl says, "It would be great if he accepted me for who I am." I tell Girl that she is looking for approval and acceptance from Boy, just as he is seeking them from her.

In this situation, Boy and Girl's issues mirrored each other. If like attracts like, we know that Boy and Girl met to work this issue out together. Girl is confused. I remind Girl that Spirit brought Boy and Girl together for a reason. I add that Spirit brought Boy into her life because he is the best soul to provide her with her growth potential at this time. This is also the reason Girl is in Boy's life. However, after Spirit arranges the initial meeting, free will and the power of choice enter the equation. At that time, Boy or Girl has the choice and the free will to accept or deny the situation. I explain to Girl that she needs to come from a place of honesty and openness in her dialogue with Boy once she makes her decision.

The story of Boy and Girl is very common. We all have issues. We all have unfinished business, incomplete stories, and places within ourselves that need healing. When entering into a relationship, we need to decide whether someone's white elephant is an issue we can embrace or must reject. Girl had a decision to make; it included two facets. Could Girl tolerate Boy's white elephant? Could Girl embrace working on her own acceptance and approval issues?

Several days later, Boy contacted Girl, as I had indicated he would. Girl, having had time to think about the white elephant concept, decided to remain neutral and see if Boy was still interested. Through a series of text messages, Boy asked Girl what she was doing for the weekend. Girl indicated she had already made plans. Girl asked why Boy hadn't contacted her in over a week. Boy said he'd been busy. Girl laughed and said that we're all busy. Girl wanted to know the real reason. Boy said he wasn't looking for anything serious. Girl said she wasn't looking for a fling. Boy said he'd talk to Girl another time and wished her the best. Girl told Boy she'd talk to him later. Girl is annoyed and frustrated. Boy is annoyed and frustrated.

When Girl called me the next day, I asked her why she hadn't come from a place of openness and honesty in her dialogue with Boy. Girl admitted she'd gone into bitchy mode. Why? Because she knew that this mode and tone would turn Boy off. Why did Girl want to turn Boy off? Because she wasn't ready to deal with his issue or her own. Girl chose to push Boy away instead of dealing with the white elephant. At that point, Boy and Girl temporarily parted ways. I explained to Girl that the situation wasn't over yet and that I felt Boy and Girl would connect again.

Relationships are gifts that serve us in two ways. First, they provide opportunities for growth and evolution. Second, relationships are our biggest teacher. In a healthy relationship, both parties are growing, evolving, and working through their issues together. A long-term relationship is successful when both parties commit to working through their "stuff." A relationship ends after a short period of time because changes in the dynamic are not embraced by both parties. Why does this happen? One party becomes complacent and stops growing. The other party continues to grow and move forward. When this occurs, a disparity blooms. Once the disparity begins, the white elephants that were previously tolerable, familiar, and part of relationship patterns are seen as negative. Why? The party that has evolved and moved forward surpasses the other party. The party that lagged behind can no longer keep up. When this rift presents itself, the inevitable happens: the fights get bigger, the words nastier, and the tears become unstoppable.

Why does one party stop growing? Why does the other party continue growing? I feel that one person stops growing because of fear of the unknown. This person doesn't know what kind of changes will result from constant growth and/or shifts, so he or she stops the flow. On an unconscious level, the person asks if continued change will eventually transform him or her into someone he or she doesn't recognize. The answer is not so simple. We do change and shift, but we always know ourselves. In fact, we learn to know ourselves on a deeper level. On the other hand, the party that continues to grow finds joy, comfort, and love in releasing old parts and pieces that don't fit anymore. The same party embraces unknown adventures and experiences with a zest for the new.

Jack and Jill had been married for twenty years. Jack and Jill raised a son and a daughter together. When their children reached the freshman and sophomore levels in college, Jack and Jill's marriage was in need of repair. Jack's neediness had worn Jill's nerves down to nothing. Their relationship hadn't always been this way. In the beginning, Jill was thrilled with the notion that Jack's world revolved around her. She was happy to satisfy all his needs. Over the years, Jill began to see that Jack's constant needs always took center stage. Jill recalled the many instances when Jack's needs had surpassed those of their children. Over time, Jill began to see Jack as selfish and self-involved. Jill also felt that in regard to her daily priorities, her own needs came last. Over the years, Jill grew unhappier each day. Finally, Jill grew to resent Jack.

Jack was confused. He worked hard, provided for Jill and, most importantly, provided for his children. Was it wrong to think that he should be the king of his castle? Jack liked it when Jill was attentive to all his needs. Lately, Jill gave Jack a hard time when he asked for his needs to be met. What had happened? Did something change? Why didn't Jill want to take care of him? Jack was unable to see that Jill had grown beyond his perception of her. In Jill's mind, Jack should begin satisfying his own needs. And Jill felt it was time to address her needs, especially since their children were now attending college.

Looking at their history, Jack's white elephant was evident to Jill from the beginning. However, Jack couldn't see, or didn't want to see, Jill's white elephant: her need to be needed. During the course of their marriage, Jill's need to be needed disappeared. Jill wasn't interested in satisfying others' needs anymore. Jill was angry about ignoring her own needs for too long. Jill was angry at Jack, but she was even angrier at herself. At this point, Jill readily turned the spotlight on herself and began doing things she wanted to do. Jack was angry because Jill had changed. Jack felt unloved and unimportant. A large white elephant now stood between Jack and Jill. After separating and getting back together twice, Jill filed for divorce from Jack. Today, Jill and Jack remain cordial to each other because of their children. Jill has continued her work with me to find the right balance between addressing her needs and being open to the needs of others. Jack has a new girlfriend who is very similar in personality to the old Jill. For Jack, the teachings continue.

KEY POINTS FOR REFLECTION AND JOURNALING

1. Do you understand the concept of a white elephant?
2. Can you understand how one partner's white elephant can mirror another's white elephant?
3. Think of a past relationship: What was the white elephant that your partner had? Can you see that issue in yourself?
4. Which white elephant is intolerable to you? Why?
5. Can you commit to working through your own white elephant while your partner works through his or hers?

A MEDITATION TO ASSIST THE JOURNEY

Find a quiet spot. Take several deep breaths. Focus on the breath going in and out of the body. Let go and release. Let go and release. Let go and release. Beginning with your toes and traveling up to the top of your head, slowly take the time to relax your body. Imagine all your stresses fading and floating away. Take several more deep breaths. When you are fully relaxed, see yourself sitting on a beautiful beach at sunset. Take another breath and allow yourself to go into a deeper place of relaxation. Just be. When you are ready, look around you. See the red ball of the sun as it begins to sink below the horizon, smell the salty air, feel the sand between your toes and hear the waves as they lap gently onto the shore. Allow yourself to feel completely at peace here. Take a moment and connect with your heart. Go deep into the most beautiful cavern of your heart and allow yourself to feel the love there. What color do you see here? Is it gold? Is it green? Is it pink? Is it luminescent? Allow that love to spiral out of your heart and wash over you from head to toe. Feel this love resonating and vibrating all around you. Take several deep breaths. Take a moment to be completely at peace. What is the most challenging white elephant you have experienced in a relationship? Why? How did you feel about this white elephant? Why did this relationship end? How would you feel about this white elephant, if it showed-up in a new relationship? Would you make different choices? Why? When you are ready, state the following:

'I am aware that every relationship has a white elephant. I am aware that the white elephant issue(s) between my partner and I can be resolved and healed over time, if we are both willing to do the work. With this knowledge, I reclaim the relationship of my dreams. I transform my energies. I shift my law of attraction qualities. I am in the proper alignment. I am grateful for the commitment I have made to myself as I walk this journey to the right relationship.'

When you are ready, return to the room and take notice of any sensations or feelings you are experiencing. If possible, take notes or record your impressions in a journal.

CHAPTER 16

THE TIME-OUT

The dictionary describes a time-out as a "brief suspension of activity, a suspension of play in an athletic game, and a quiet period used as a disciplinary measure for children." Time-outs are beneficial in our dating lives as well. A time-out in our dating lives is about relaxing, having fun, and allowing for rejuvenation. Many times when I suggest that a client take a time-out from dating, I'm looked at with disapproving eyes. Why is it that people shudder at the thought of not being an active member of the dating pool? We seem to believe that if we aren't in the dating pool we might miss someone or something. What exactly are we missing? Bad dates with the wrong people?

The misconception that we need to be constantly dating or attempting to date is very deceiving. Society has conditioned us this way, and so we do not believe in allowing for a break from time to time. However, time-outs between relationships are vital.

Time-outs allow us to heal, review our mistakes, forgive ourselves, forgive our partner's mistakes, rest, recharge our batteries, gain perspective on what we want, and achieve clarity.

Recently, I told Sara that she needed a time-out. After getting over the shock of the idea of not being an active fish in the sea, she asked when a new love interest would arrive. I explained to Sara that I didn't see anyone new coming into her life for five or six months.

"Five or six months?"

I thought she was going to have a panic attack. I told her a time-out during this period would enable her to be ready for the new situation when it presented itself. Sara balked. She didn't want to be stagnant for five or six months. She wanted to be actively engaged in the dating pool. I asked her if there was anything she had wanted to do but hadn't done because she was focused on dating. She indicated she'd been thinking of taking a yoga class and that she wanted to try ceramics. She explained that a friend was learning how to ride a motorcycle, and while she felt it was dangerous, she also thought it might be fun. I encouraged Sara to give these new hobbies a try. While Sara seemed okay with the hobby concept, she still could not wrap her head around the five- or six-month period she'd be out of the dating scene.

"Do you know what you want in a relationship?" I asked her.

"Yes — a nice guy," she said.

"That's not clear enough," I told her. I explained that she needed to be more specific and have more clarity about what and who she was looking for. I added that a time-out was a great space for gaining that clarity. I explained the importance of focusing her thoughts, energies, and attention on her inner self during this time-out period. I encouraged her to look at her previous relationships to see where she had made mistakes, where she had been disappointed, where she could have behaved or acted differently. Finally, I added that a time-out was vital for giving her spirit and her soul space to renew. Once renewed, Sara would have a stronger connection with her divine self.

If you've seen a deck of tarot cards, you know that the tarot is divided into two sections: the major arcana and the minor arcana. The major arcana details the journey of the Fool and his travels. The Fool travels from one card to the other, similar to the way we move from one phase to another in life and in relationships. Almost halfway through the major arcana is a card called the Hermit. The Hermit represents the time in the Fool's journey to go inward, a period of introspection, self-analysis, and solitude. In the period of the Hermit, we go within, reflect on our choices, look at our lessons; we review the teachings we've mastered and the ones that still need work. While the Hermit card artwork varies from deck to deck, the interesting thing about the Hermit card is that he is always pictured in scenes related to wandering and searching. He is usually shown holding a lantern and looking toward the darkness. The lantern is symbolic of its ability to light our path into the unknown. The Hermit represents a time of being alone and remaining solitary; this space is also about allowing the dust to settle so we can gain clarity. As a society, we are always busy, consumed, and stressed. As a result of this, our body, our vessel, becomes cloudy and unsettled. We never step into or out of the Hermit period the same person. We emerge shifted, altered — ready to embrace what Spirit will gift to us.

Additionally, the Hermit allows us an amazing space to shed what no longer serves us. The Hermit provides us with the space to be with ourselves, remember our uniqueness, and reconnect with the Divine on many levels. Finally, the Hermit allows us to see that our cup, or vessel, should be empty in order to live fulfilled lives. Slowing down, allowing, and letting wisdom come into our being provides this knowledge.

Knowing the power of the Hermit, I'm fascinated by the typical reluctance to step into that space. My client, although willing to try a few new things, was not willing to embrace the Hermit. She wasn't interested in accepting the gift such inner work could provide.

From my experiences with clients, reasons why we resist the Hermit include:

- We are too occupied with the outer world and the sense of purpose and connection we receive from it.
- We are too occupied with technology and social media — iPhones, the Internet, instant messaging, Facebook, and Twitter keep us constantly focused on what is happening in other's lives instead of looking at our own life.
- We resist our inner terrain and tapestry because it's often ugly, messy, and painful. We want to avoid the pain, so we "don't go there." We take the attitude that the pain didn't happen or doesn't exist.

As a society we often push down, shove away, disregard, or turn a blind eye to our hurts and disappointments. In doing so, we avoid the deeper connection we can develop with ourselves and Spirit. This deepening comes about as a result of acknowledging or owning these hurts and disappointments and embracing their teachings.

In my own experiences with the Hermit, I have emerged feeling like a completely different person. I've looked in the mirror and observed more peace in my face, I've experienced more joy in my walk, and I've felt an amazing level of connection with Spirit that I couldn't have imagined existed. My vessel is always emptier when I emerge from the Hermit. The journey into and out of the Hermit has always proven beneficial to me because of my willingness to embrace the shift that comes with it.

Another tarot card that is beneficial during the time-out phase is the Death card. The Death card doesn't always mean someone is dying (though in specific situations it can). The Death card is about releasing, letting go, and surrendering those parts of ourselves that no longer serve us. We die to our old selves. If you have always perceived your role in relationships in a certain way, the Death card can represent the space within which you release, shift, or let go of that perception in order to allow another one to emerge. The Death card allows us to rebirth ourselves.

The Death card is usually pictured as a skeleton or a grim reaper holding a scythe. Scythes are typically known for weeding, reaping, or harvesting. In this image, the scythe is used because the skeleton, or grim reaper, is harvesting what is no longer needed. The Death card allows the "old" us to give up what no longer serves our journey to make space for what will assist our journey as we are reborn into a new self.

When Sara contacted me a few months later, I asked her if she had embraced the Hermit. She indicated that she had taken a yoga class and liked it, but she hadn't gone back. She had also signed up for a four-week pottery class; she'd only attended twice. She thought the pottery class was fun, but she couldn't connect with any of the students in her class. She said that she tried motorcycle riding but found it too nerve-wracking and dangerous. Finally, she said that she'd been hitting the clubs and casually dating, but she was holding off on anything serious until the right guy came into the picture, as I'd previously indicated would happen.

I asked Sara if she'd gained any clarity about what she wanted in a relationship. She told me she was still looking for that nice guy.

Sara inquired about the new man she'd be meeting. She got excited when I gave her a description of what he looked like. It was evident that Sara had resisted her time-out. Since she wasn't willing to do the inner work, would she be happy with the new man she met? Would it be the right relationship for her?

A few weeks later Dave contacted me; he'd been thinking about taking a four- to five-month reprieve from dating to "get his head together." When I inquired about Dave's need to get his head together, he told me that he was meeting the same "rescue-me" type of woman over and over. And Dave felt the break would get him on track with his dissertation work and its impending deadline. Dave and I discussed his attitude toward the rescue-me types. Upon reflection, Dave admitted that he disliked their neediness. However, he also realized that he found some comfort in their presence. He felt their need to be rescued gave him an upper hand, but Dave was frustrated because he felt he gave more than he received. During our work together, Dave thought a lot about what an ideal relationship would be like. Additionally, I asked him to review his past relationships so he could get a feel for what had gone wrong, see his teachings, learn his lessons, etc. I also asked Dave to put together lists regarding his ideal and deal-breaker traits for a new love. After compiling his lists, Dave began working with them. Dave also spent his time-out reacquainting himself with his guitar. Dave explained that he had been an avid player all throughout school, but he hadn't kept up with practicing and playing once he'd entered his doctoral program. Between the work on his dissertation, guitar practice, and his soul searching during the Hermit phase, Dave emerged from his time-out ready to embrace the dating scene. In my last session with Dave, he told me about his new relationship and explained the peace he felt at not having to deal with the drama of the rescue-me types any longer. As you can see, Dave was on track for the next steps along his romantic journey.

KEY POINTS FOR REFLECTION AND JOURNALING

1. Do you understand the concept of a time-out?
2. Can you comprehend the benefits of taking a three-, six-, or nine-month time-out from dating?
3. What is your biggest resistance to taking a time-out? Why?
4. Can you see the correlation between the hermit mode and your ability to go deeper?
5. Do you understand the connection between time-out mode and the death card?

A MEDITATION TO ASSIST THE JOURNEY

Find a quiet spot. Take several deep breaths. Focus on the breath going in and out of the body. Let go and release. Let go and release. Let go and release. Beginning with your toes and traveling up to the top of your head, slowly take the time to relax your body. Imagine all your stresses fading and floating away. Take several more deep breaths. When you are fully relaxed, see yourself sitting on a beautiful beach at sunset. Take another breath and allow yourself to go into a deeper place of relaxation. Just be. When you are ready, look around you. See the red ball of the sun as it begins to sink below the horizon, smell the salty air, feel the sand between your toes and hear the waves as they lap gently onto the shore. Allow yourself to feel completely at peace here. Take a moment and connect with your heart. Go deep into the most beautiful cavern of your heart and allow yourself to feel the love there. What color do you see here? Is it gold? Is it green? Is it pink? Is it luminescent? Allow that love to spiral out of your heart and wash over you from head to toe. Feel this love resonating and vibrating all around you. Take several deep breaths. Take a moment to be completely at peace. Take a few moments to connect with your feelings about time-outs. How do you feel about taking a time-out? Are you open? Are you resistant? Are there new hobbies or pursuits that you have wanted to try? Have you put-off these hobbies or pursuits? Would you be willing to embrace them during a time-out phase? If you are resistant to taking a time-out, take a moment and breathe deeply into your feelings. What do those feelings say to you? Do they tell you that you do not need to take a break? Do they tell you that you are missing dating opportunities? Do they prompt you to keep at it? Can you see the meaning behind these feelings? When you are ready, state the following:

'I am aware of the importance of time-outs. I am aware that they allow me time to gain perspective and insight into previous relationships. I am at peace with the concept of taking a time-out. During a time-out, I choose to fill my life with new hobbies and pursuits. I choose to use this time to find out what I truly want in the relationship of my dreams. I know that this time-out will help me to reclaim the relationship of my dreams. I transform my energies. I shift my law of attraction qualities. I am in the proper alignment. I am grateful for the commitment I have made to myself as I walk this journey to the right relationship.'

When you are ready, return to the room and take notice of any sensations or feelings you are experiencing. If possible, take notes or record your impressions in a journal.

CHAPTER 17

THE LISTS

I believe that most people go to a psychic with the same question: How do I meet Mr. Right or Ms. Right? I have often heard the statement, "I'd love to meet someone new and exciting!" When I ask about the qualities they are looking for in someone special, most people say they'd like to meet someone nice. Hmm! Someone nice? That is all you are looking for?

The missing component here is clarity. We need to have clarity about what we truly want in a relationship. To help clients obtain their ideal relationship, I have developed a system called the lists, which are divided into two categories. The first is called the desired list, a list of the top twenty-five qualities that your ideal partner must have. Examples might include a dynamic personality, a working professional who earns a good living, a vegetarian, an animal lover, an avid reader, a person who works out regularly and takes care of him- or herself, a lover of history, fine arts, etc. The desired list can start out with your top fifty, seventy-five, or one hundred qualities, but eventually it needs to be pared down to twenty-five. The desired list is vital because it helps clients become clear about what they truly want from a new partner.

The law of attraction has taught us that we are constantly attracting what we vibrate. This law shows us that we need to be aware of what we are vibrating because this vibration attracts new people and situations into our energy field all the time. The reason why the desired list is so important is because it provides us with clarity in order to draw in the right relationship. Compiling the desired list is no easy task. In many cases, clients take weeks to compile their list. In creating the list, thoroughness is very important. You don't want to attract the wrong lover, do you?

From time to time, clients will come for a session to review their desired list. Recently, a client came for a session and presented me with her desired list. As I scanned the list, the word *health* was screaming in my ear. Finally I said to her, "He looks like a great guy on paper, but is he dead?" She looked at me strangely. "You don't indicate health or well-being at all. Are you hoping to date a ghost?" I said. Immediately, she realized that she'd forgotten to ask for her new partner to be healthy. While this quality may seem obvious, it is important when compiling the list to cover all the bases. Do you want to attract the man or woman or your dreams and then discover he or she is ill?

Another time I was listening to a client's list over the phone. She mentioned something about her new love wanting a family. I stopped her and asked if she was referring to children. She said yes. I explained that everyone's definition of family is different and that if she wanted children she needed to specify children. Because of the vagueness of her statement, she might have ended up with a guy who wanted a loving, warm family but didn't want children.

A male client said, "Well, I want her to be sweet and nice." I told him that was great, but I asked him if he wanted her to have a career. "I don't care what she does for a living," he said. I explained that he needed to be clear about whether she had a career or not. I added that a lack of clarity would bring him someone who was very sweet but who could be poor or homeless. Again this trait may seem obvious, but the universe gives us what we ask for. Period! We can't just assume someone has a career, if we don't ask that they have one. We can't expect the universe to say, "Well, he didn't ask that she have a career, but I'm sure he wants her to have one." The universe doesn't work that way.

As you can see, the most important thing about the list is to *be specific!* I tell clients that they need to have a vision of what they want, and then they need to put those items on the list. The client needs to visualize Mr. Right or Ms. Right in their mind's eye and then translate his or her qualities to the desired list. While being specific is important, there is no need for over-specificity — for example, indicating that she must have blue eyes or he must be from New York City. Such over-specificity is unnecessary.

Once the desired list is created, tweaked, and reviewed over and over and over and over and over and *over*, the time comes to make the second list, what I call the deal breakers — qualities in a partner that are 100 percent unacceptable in a relationship with you. Common and obvious deal breakers include abusers, addicts, someone who is poor or broke, mean or angry, mentally unstable, has served time in jail, etc. While most of these seem obvious, others are unique to specific people. One of my deal breakers is smoking. I will not date a smoker. *Period!* He could be the nicest guy in the world, but if he smokes he's off my desired list. To divorced clients who are done raising children, the thought of dating a man or women who has young kids or wants kids is a deal breaker. One of my male clients told me that he wants a woman with a viable career. To him, the woman needs to bring financial stability to the relationship, just as he does. In his words, she needs to be providing fifty-fifty. "If she wants me to provide 100 percent of her financial needs, she's just given me a deal breaker," he said.

When compiling your deal-breaker list, remember that deal breakers vary depending on what your goals for your desired relationship are. For one woman, a man who is divorced with kids is a catch. In her mind, this shows a man who has committed once and will commit again under the right circumstances. To another woman, that man and his children are a deal breaker. To one man, a woman who drinks two glasses of wine after a busy day at the office is attempting to relax and unwind. To another man, that woman has a drinking problem that will lead her to drink more and more when life presents additional challenges. The same man may wonder why she isn't meditating, doing cardio, or taking yoga classes to reduce stress. As you can see, creating a specific deal-breaker list is just as important as a specific desired list.

By this point, you have prepared the lists, and the preparation has brought you clarity about what you want and don't want. The time has come to start working the desired list. You do not need to work your deal-breaker list. The purpose of that list is to provide clarity on what isn't wanted.

How do you work your desired list? You read it aloud to the universe first thing in the morning and several times throughout the day. You read it aloud to yourself during lunch time and during your afternoon snack. Don't just read it like you would read your grocery list. Read your list with intention and conviction. Read it with the commitment to making this list become a reality. Read it like an actor who is so convincing that she gets the part. Work the list!

Why is it so important to work the list? The more often you read the list — and read it and read it — the more your vibration changes. The more often you read the list aloud to the universe, the more you believe that you can have what is on the list and the more you feel worthy of the qualities on the list. The more you read it, the stronger your belief grows. The stronger your beliefs, the greater the likelihood you will be in alignment for truly getting what you want. When you become the list, you and the list merge energetically.

Another important facet of working the list is visualization. During this process, you need to visualize your ideal partner. A combination of reading and visualizing will bring your desire to you. The easy part is when the universe says, "Ah, now I see what she or he wants. Let me bring it to her or him." This is the way the law of attraction works. We need to be clear about what we want. We need to believe we are worthy of having what we want. We need to ask for what we want over and over until we are in alignment with it. As we become in alignment with it, our vibration changes to bring us in harmony with what we want. When we are in alignment with our desire, the universe delivers it to us. Yes, it is that simple.

Compiling the list and working the list require a lot of energy, time, and focus. This is a task that pays off, if we commit to the outcome. However, our society and the way in which many of us are conditioned lead many people to fall off the track during the process. I have had clients compile the list and then call me two months later and say, "Well, where is he?" or "Why hasn't he arrived in my life?" My answer is always two-fold. "Have you been working the list?" I ask.

"Yeah, I read it three times a day for a few weeks, and now I just pick it up here and there."

"How do you expect this list to work if you aren't working it?" I ask.

At this point, the excuses appear. "Well, I forget to do it, and then I'm in the shower, and I can't read it while I'm driving to work, can I? That's dangerous! I'll have a car accident." Excuses and more excuses.

"How badly do you want that relationship?" I ask.

At this point, there is silence. The client knows she has not kept up her end of the bargain. I explain that she has to commit working the list or it won't happen. Secondly, I ask if she feels ready for what she wants.

"Oh, yes, I'm ready to meet him."

At that point, I will get an intuitive hit about something else. I can see why she is in this place. For example, she is still in touch with her ex, hasn't forgiven her mother for abandonment issues, or hasn't been doing the work to feel good about herself. She is stuck. At this point, the client either gives up on the list or takes the initiative to do the work needed in order to get in alignment with his or her desire.

Human nature, Hollywood endings, and the desire for companionship lead us to ask for the right relationship to come into our lives. Unfortunately, somewhere along the way we decide we don't want to do the work. Why? I've asked myself that question a million times. We want the end result, but we don't want to do the work to get ourselves there. Because we live in a reality that is dictated by our belief system and what we feel we are worthy of, a lot of people end up never getting their ideal relationship because they quit before they find the joy that is waiting for them.

When you do the inner work and work the list, you will find the right person. I've seen it happen to those clients who commit to having the dream relationship they've always wanted. Like everything else in life, the journey to obtaining the relationship of your dreams starts and ends with you.

KEY POINTS FOR REFLECTION AND JOURNALING

1. Do you understand the importance of being clear about your desired relationship?

2. At this moment, do you know what you want in a desired relationship? Are you willing to take the time to get clarity?

3. Can you commit to making a desired list?

4. Can you commit to making a deal-breaker list?

5. Are you willing to work the desired list, shift your vibration, and change what you need to change about yourself in order to find the right partner? How much time and energy are you willing to give?

A MEDITATION TO ASSIST THE JOURNEY

Find a quiet spot. Take several deep breaths. Focus on the breath going in and out of the body. Let go and release. Let go and release. Let go and release. Beginning with your toes and traveling up to the top of your head, slowly take the time to relax your body. Imagine all your stresses fading and floating away. Take several more deep breaths. When you are fully relaxed, see yourself sitting on a beautiful beach at sunset. Take another breath and allow yourself to go into a deeper place of relaxation. Just be. When you are ready, look around you. See the red ball of the sun as it begins to sink below the horizon, smell the salty air, feel the sand between your toes and hear the waves as they lap gently onto the shore. Allow yourself to feel completely at peace here. Take a moment and connect with your heart. Go deep into the most beautiful cavern of your heart and allow yourself to feel the love there. What color do you see here? Is it gold? Is it green? Is it pink? Is it luminescent? Allow that love to spiral out of your heart and wash over you from head to toe. Feel this love resonating and vibrating all around you. Take several deep breaths. Take a moment to be completely at peace. Envision yourself on that special day when you are about to marry the partner of your dreams. How do you feel? Look at your journey to this day. What were your frustrations, anxieties and aggravations? Can you see the divineness of this journey? Now bring yourself back to the present. Are you ready for this journey? Focus on your partner. What does he or she look like? How do you feel when you are around him or her? What are his or her personality traits? What are the wonderful things he or she does for you? What are the wonderful things you do for him or her? What does his or her love feel like? What does the love you have for him or her feel like? Why do you want to marry this person? Why does he or she want to marry you? When you are ready, state the following:

'I know that my special day is waiting for me. However, I am aware that I must heal and make peace with my inner landscape. I am aware that I must work my list in order to change my law of attraction. I am aware that the journey to I do begins with my commitment to myself. I know I can have the relationship of my dreams. Today I claim the relationship of my dreams. I know that a divine relationship is waiting for me. I choose that relationship. In choosing that relationship, I transform my energies. I am in the proper alignment. I am grateful for this journey and my commitment to a loving, beautiful, supportive relationship that will assist me in evolving my soul.'

When you are ready, return to the room and take notice of any sensations or feelings you are experiencing. If possible, take notes or record your impressions in a journal.

Made in the USA
Charleston, SC
20 February 2013